PRAISE FOR C[...]

"Jim McComas is a trial lawyer extraordinaire with skills that amaze even the most polished trial attorneys. In *Case Analysis,* McComas shares the secrets of his notable successes in fighting for the underdog. With clarity and detail, McComas teaches us how to win the hard cases against an over-resourced opponent. In *Case Analysis,* we have found the Ark of the Covenant in trial law."

—Ronald S. Sullivan Jr., professor, Harvard Law School, director of the Harvard Trial Advocacy Workshop and the Harvard Criminal Justice Institute

"In *Case Analysis,* Jim McComas uses his tremendous skills as a lawyer and educator to provide clear, concise instructions on how to dissect and understand those seemingly impossible cases—and win! *Case Analysis* is an insightful, step-by-step blueprint for lawyers to understand and plan for a successful verdict in those cases where the facts, the law, and more appear to be against you."

—Penny Marshall, former chief federal defender for the U.S. District of Delaware, former president of the Association of Federal Defenders

"*Case Analysis* is a 'must-read.' Author Jim McComas translates his phenomenal track record into a brilliant step-by-step method for building your case while undoing the opposition's."

—Jo-Ann Wallace, president and CEO of the National Legal Aid & Defender Association (NLADA)

"*Case Analysis* focuses on our trial presentation to the jury, our only audience, and the real life information they need to come back with the right verdict. During the years I worked with Jim McComas as an investigator and trial assistant, I saw this method put to use in impossible cases with amazing, unbelievable results."

—Monique Rapuzzi, independent investigator

"Jim McComas is a genius in the courtroom, but he also can translate his winning ways to the page. Read this book, and you will learn what works with juries and why it works, whether you are trying civil or criminal cases, and whether you are just beginning your trial practice or have been at it for years."

—Mark Rochon, criminal defense attorney,
former chief of the Trial Division at the Public
Defender Service for the District of Columbia

"This book is a must-read for trial lawyers. It reminds us that trials are won by thorough Case Analysis and provides a clear, organized method for evaluating the strengths and weaknesses of any case."

—Jamie Gardner, litigation partner, Patton Boggs, LLP,
and instructor in clinical programs at
Harvard and Georgetown Law Schools

Case Analysis

Winning Hard Cases against the Odds

James H. McComas

Trial Guides

Trial Guides, LLC

Trial Guides, LLC, Portland, Oregon 97205

Printed in the United States of America

ISBN: 978-1-934833-48-3

Library of Congress Control Number 2011941978

Trial Guides, LLC
Attn: Permissions
2400 SW Park Place
Portland, OR 97205
(800) 309-6845
www.trialguides.com

Interior design by Laura Lind Design

Jacket design by Theodore Marshall

This book is printed on acid-free paper.

Contents

Author's Note

The examples in this book are derived from actual cases, in all of which I participated. However, the example cases often consist of composites of several cases. Moreover, the names of all litigants, witnesses, and counsel and other identifying details have been changed. For these reasons, any similarity between the fictionalized names, and other particulars in this book, and real individuals, companies, and cases is strictly coincidental.

Publisher's Note

This book is intended for practicing attorneys. It does not offer legal or psychological advice and does not take the place of consultation with an attorney or other professional with appropriate expertise and experience.

Attorneys are strongly cautioned to evaluate the information, ideas, and opinions set forth in this book in light of their own research, experience, and judgment; to consult applicable rules, regulations, procedures, cases, and statutes (including those issued after the publication date of this book); and to make independent decisions about whether and how to apply such information, ideas, and opinions to a particular case.

Quotations from cases, pleadings, discovery, and other sources are for illustrative purposes only and may not be suitable for use in litigation in any particular case.

As set forth in the Author's Note, the cases described in this book are composites, and the names and other identifying details of participants, litigants, witnesses, and counsel (other than the author of this book) have been fictionalized except where otherwise expressly stated by the author.

All references to the trademarks of third parties are strictly informational and for purposes of commentary. No sponsorship or endorsement by, or affiliation with, the trademark owners is claimed or implied by the author or publisher of this book.

The author and publisher disclaim any liability or responsibility for loss or damage resulting from the use of this book or the information, ideas, or opinions contained in this book.

Foreword by Jonathan A. Rapping

Seven years ago, I resigned from my position as the training director for The Public Defender Service (PDS) in Washington, DC, to move to Georgia. A new statewide effort was under way to reform indigent defense, and I was recruited to develop and run training programs for that effort. In July 2005, we held a weeklong trial advocacy program for the state's public defenders in Athens, Georgia. Eager to put together a great program, I invited the best trial lawyers I knew to serve as faculty. They came from a variety of states throughout the country. Their ages ranged from thirty-something to sixty-something. They included men and women. They were African American, Caucasian, and Latino. But what they all had in common was that they learned to be trial lawyers at PDS. Their tenures at PDS spanned four decades. Most did not overlap with one another at PDS. But all were close friends and colleagues. The public defenders who attended the program watched these lawyers teach and were amazed that a group of people who seemingly had little in common, apart from having at some point worked in the same public defender office, could each be such outstanding advocates.

What was it about PDS that consistently produced such phenomenal trial lawyers? Coupled with an uncompromising client-centered perspective, the answer lies largely in the way we were taught to approach our cases. We all learned that cases are won and lost long before the trial begins. That one begins earning not-guilty verdicts the moment he or she gets the case. That the ability to perform well is intricately connected to the process of Case Analysis. It is an art that was honed at PDS and passed down among the generations by one man who was among that faculty. He is the author of this book. Through this book, he passes this critical methodology on to each reader. What public defenders across Georgia witnessed that week was largely the fruit of the genius of Jim McComas.

Over the last seven years, I have had the great fortune to work with public defenders across the country. Many are committed and talented lawyers. But far too often, the quality of the lawyer is measured by his or her ability to very quickly identify winning cases and to effectively "shoot from the hip" in the courtroom. I have heard defenders brag that they can differentiate winning cases from losers simply by reading the police report, viewing this as a positive skill nurtured through experience. Others have boasted of being able to pick up a file and try the case the next day, as if this "ability" is the hallmark of a true trial jock.

While these attitudes are extreme, and likely not embraced by anyone who chooses to enrich his or her practice by reading this book, many lawyers hold them to varying degrees. Assessing the likelihood of success without putting in the work required to accurately make that prediction, and overreliance on the degree to which pure trial skill is responsible for winning cases, impede many of us from maximizing our chances of success. They are self-imposed limitations, and as Jim tells us in this book, "The greatest limits on advocacy are always self-imposed." This book helps us understand exactly why this mind-set is a self-imposed limitation and provides a methodology for freeing ourselves of these psychological shackles.

In this book, Jim warns against thinking like a lawyer and urges us to remember that our clients' fates lie in the hands of jurors. These are laypeople who employ common sense shaped by the world around them. Jurors are moved by facts and feelings, not by law. When we understand this lesson, we can begin to identify those facts and perceptions that most move jurors. They are present in every case. Some have the power to move the jury to our side. Others, to do the opposite.

Our ability to identify these "outcome levers," as Jim calls them, is the first step toward a successful trial strategy. They are often not immediately apparent in the always lacking narrative of the police reports. We must discover them through investigation, discovery, and pretrial litigation. Our ability to analyze all sides of how these outcome levers will impact our jurors is the next step, essential to incorporating them into the most viable defense theory. Our ability to maximize the impact of those outcome levers that support our theory of innocence, and to minimize those that help our opponent, is the final step. Jim teaches that this is done through our motions strategy, voir dire, opening statements, cross-examination, direct examination, jury instructions, and closing argument. Everything we do in the courtroom is driven by a strategy to maximize our outcome levers and to minimize theirs.

The Case Analysis method depends on trial preparation for its success. It teaches that the best trial lawyers must also be wonderful investigators. They must excel at pretrial litigation. They must develop a creative and aggressive discovery practice. They must master the applicable law for any given case. The lawyer who files boilerplate motions, engages in routinized discovery, relies solely on standard jury instructions, or fails to direct the investigative process will miss opportunities to identify and develop outcome levers. The best trial lawyers are masters of all these skills. They are each as much a part of the trial as the devastating cross-examination or the eloquent closing argument. In fact, these "trial practice" high points come directly from the lawyer's Case Analysis. As a matter of fact, these "trial practice" aspects of the trial depend on the lawyer's proficiency in these other areas for their success. When the lawyer who excels in all preparation and trial areas applies the Case Analysis method described in this book, his or her power to move a jury is unparalleled.

Jim came to understand this lesson early in his career as a public defender. As the person responsible for training lawyers at PDS, he began passing these lessons on to the lawyers he trained. As the head of the Trial Division, he continued to spread this message. For the twenty-three years since he left PDS, Jim has returned to teach this invaluable lesson to every lawyer who came through PDS after him.

Case Analysis has become part of being an effective trial lawyer at PDS. It works! It answers the question that continually came up in Athens that week in July 2005: "What was it about PDS that consistently produced such phenomenal trial lawyers?"

This book gives every reader the insight required to apply this method to each case. It will change the way each reader approaches representation.

Jim tells us that every case can be won, that we just have to have the courage and discipline to win it. He reminds us that we can be outspent, but never outworked or outthought. He gives us a process through which we can find a way to win that hard case. It requires discipline. It requires thoughtfulness. It requires hard work. But, as Jim reminds us, it is free. Thanks for your gift, Jim, and for sharing it so broadly.

—Jonathan A. Rapping

Jonathan A. Rapping is the founder and CEO of the Southern Public Defender Training Center, an organization dedicated to recruiting, training, and mentoring public defenders across the South in an effort to groom a new generation of defenders who will raise the standard of representation in the region. He is also an associate professor of law and the founding director of the Criminal Justice Honors Program at Atlanta's John Marshall Law School.

Mr. Rapping started his career at The Public Defender Service for the District of Columbia, where he later served as training director. He left PDS to become the training director for Georgia's then-new statewide public defender system. He subsequently spent a year in New Orleans, building its training and recruitment programs in an effort to help reform the public defender system there in the wake of Hurricane Katrina. He has trained, supervised, and mentored hundreds of public defenders across the country.

Acknowledgments

Thanks from the get-go to my mentor and close friend W. Gary Kohlman, who taught me how to pay attention and search unceasingly for opportunities in trial. And to my brothers-by-choice—my law school, then DC Public Defender Service (PDS) colleagues—Jimmy Klein and Prof. Charles Ogletree, for their decades of friendship, loyalty, and support. Thanks to the amazing women who co-counseled trials with me in DC: Avis Buchanan, Angela "Amani" Davis, Syrie Davis, Penny Marshall, Rita Pendry, and Kim Taylor, as well as the awesome advocate Michele Roberts, who succeeded me as Trial Chief. Thanks also to Jonathan Rapping, the outstanding trainer now tirelessly helping Southern lawyers bring quality representation to their indigent clients. And to all the other lawyers who have done the hardest work at PDS, for their great friendship, loyalty, and effort, both when I was there and since then, as I've had the privilege of seeing them in training every year since 1988.

Then there's twenty years in Alaska, where I met three great lawyers who became dear friends: Rick Friedman, to whose firm I was *Of Counsel* for ten years, who encouraged me for decades to write this book; Cindy Strout, who tried fascinating murder cases with me throughout the vast lawless stretches of the last frontier; and Phil Weidner, who never asks for, or grants, any quarter. Also, thanks to my special plaintiff's-case consultants, attorneys Kirsten Friedman and Lesley Zork.

Thanks to my mother and father, Hazelyn and Harrold McComas, for providing the intellectual environment and education opportunities that made my career possible. And thanks to my dear friend Brian Long, who helps me maintain some sort of balance in my life by sharing with me his intimate knowledge of the wildness of northern Wisconsin.

Finally, and now, at last, once again first in the line of my focus and attention, I want to thank my remarkable wife of thirty-seven years, Anne, and my sons, Dan and Henry, for allowing me to pursue the consuming trial work I did for thirty years and for filling my life with love, humor, and excitement along the way. I treasure every moment.

Introduction

This book contains the "keys to the kingdom" of much greater success in trial litigation. It provides the best method to identify what determines outcomes in trial cases and to develop the factual substance necessary to maximize our chances of winning. Outstanding criminal defense attorneys throughout the United States have validated these brave claims with decades of practice.

We never enjoy a resource advantage over our adversaries. To the contrary, prosecution systems typically have enormous resource advantages in litigation. So, we have to use what is available to even—and then overcome—the odds. Thinking is free, and effective Case Analysis is where good lawyers for the underdog turn the tide.

We can also work harder than our opponents—a fact that can improve our odds and demoralize the other side. And we can care more. Because our clients are people, not institutions, and because our representation is always thoroughly client based, our emotional connection to the actual people we represent is a powerful motivating force. Let the other side make jokes about "true believers"—the fact is, they are confused and frightened by the strength of our commitment to our clients.

Where did this method of Case Analysis come from? I had the privilege of working for the first eight years of my practice at

The Public Defender Service for the District of Columbia (PDS). There, I learned a tradition of excellent, client-based representation. I followed PDS's initial, full-time, six-week training program with four years of felony trials and a hugely informative year in appeals. I developed this method in my fifth year, when I wrote and conducted the training program for the incoming class of ten lawyers, with an experience range of zero to five years practice. Revising the whole curriculum for this class required that I consciously focus on what we did and why it worked (or, in some cases, didn't).

The big breakthrough, however, came in my seventh and eighth years, when I served as Chief of the Trial Division. A typical day would require that I listen to, and give feedback on, other attorneys' opening statements, proposed cross-examinations, and closing arguments before court started. Then I observed key portions of many of the serious felony trials our office had going across the street in Superior Court. Hours of consulting with lawyers about investigation, preparation, motions work, and trial planning followed. Evenings meant going with our lawyers to the jail, doing mock cross-examinations of our clients to see if they should testify, and preparing them if they were going to do so. I devoted weekends to more of the same, minus the court observation.

In short, I had the unique—and invaluable—opportunity to be personally involved at crucial points in hundreds of serious felony cases. The Public Defender Service tried over two hundred of those cases in those two years, and the verdicts gave me immediate insight into what worked and what didn't. The result was the method of Case Analysis described in this book. Ever since I left PDS, they have asked me to return every year to do a day of training on the subject of Case Analysis for the new, incoming lawyers. Every year since 1988, I have done so. The purpose of this book is to share this approach with a much wider audience of dedicated trial lawyers.

By the time of trial, we know a vast amount of information about our cases but will only present a small portion to the jury. The core insight is that, within that small portion, only a few facts and circumstances determine the outcome for either side.

Accordingly, our task is to functionally analyze the case in order to identify those few points that can determine the outcome, and which we will call *outcome levers,* on either side of the case. Once we have found the outcome levers, our job is to eliminate or minimize the prosecution's points, while maximizing ours. With this understanding of what really matters, we select the defense theory that best fits our outcome analysis. Finally, we create our story: a plausible, persuasive, factual reality of our client's innocence.

This book proceeds with the following organization:

Chapter 1, "The Primary Case Example," covers the case *State v. Peter Piper.* I use this example to illustrate the method of Case Analysis in later sections.

Chapter 2, "Determine the Outcome," identifies and uses the small number of circumstances in every case that can determine the outcome for either side. It also helps us identify the "trapdoors," through which an otherwise-successful presentation can fall to failure.

The thinking in chapter 2 requires us to scrutinize the whole case and all of its components, in order to find the parts of the case that are especially important. This may be a branch on a tree of fact in the factual forest or some phenomenon having nothing to do with facts at all. Once we identify the outcome levers for each side, we must find and use all the legal, factual, and advocacy tools that can eliminate or minimize the prosecution's levers, and maximize the impact of our own. The final step is to develop a summary case theory that factually and legally implements the understanding we have attained from the preceding steps.

In chapter 3, "Develop the Facts—Create a Plausible, Persuasive Reality," we develop a highly detailed reality of the events. This is both plausible and persuasive and shows the client's factual and legal innocence. This analysis encourages us to become aware of the huge amount of maneuvering room that exists in the facts of any case. This vastness enables us to develop a plausible, persuasive reality that will produce the desired outcome.

We repeat this Case Analysis, reevaluate it, and modify it throughout the representation, from first impressions when we pick up the case, through the pretrial preparation and litigation stages, and all the way through the actual trial. New information, rulings on motions, and events in the courtroom or community can all alter how effective our thinking was before we discovered them or before the events occurred. Typically, our own understanding develops over time, and our Case Analysis must develop with it.

Chapter 4, "Tips to Prepare and Organize the Case," provides simple checklists to go through when preparing for trial.

Chapter 5, "Maxims for Attorneys for the Underdog," consists of thirty-two truths about representing accused people and trying cases. Their purpose is to provoke thinking and discussion as well as provide some inspiration for those who do this hard work.

Chapter 6, "Conclusion," is a final explanation of how this Case Analysis method is integral to every stage of preparing for and conducting litigation.

The appendices contain short discussions and long examples of some of the actual tools we can use to eliminate or minimize the opponent's outcome levers and maximize the impact of our own. Sample voir dire questions, motions to admit other crimes or bad acts evidence against witnesses, and to exclude it against our client, a Notice of Expert, and some demonstrably effective special jury instructions are all referenced in the text and are included in the appendices.

1

The Primary Case Example

State v. Peter Piper

The following case scenario appears throughout the book as an example. This example appears to be a simple, straightforward, prosecution-loaded criminal case. However, when we analyze it effectively, it produces a multitude of opportunities for a successful defense.[1]

Here's the case:

Peter Piper (PP) is in trouble again in Anytown. He has juvenile adjudications for Robbery-1 (three years ago) and Manslaughter (thirty months ago). He was committed to kiddie jail—the Troubled Youth Center (TYC)—and released after eighteen months, having been a model prisoner. PP is an African American teen, about five foot ten, handsome, slim, muscular, and dark skinned. He has a slight black mustache, very short

1. This example is based on an actual case that I tried in the early 1980s. Cross-examinations of the two most significant witnesses in this case—both of which are rooted in the Case Analysis below—appear in my book *Dynamic Cross-Examination: A Whole New Way to Create Opportunities to Win* (2011).

black hair, and "TYC Members Only" tattooed on the back of his left hand.

Now, barely eighteen, PP is in critical condition in the hospital, the result of a gunshot wound inflicted by white shopkeeper Quarrel Kwiktrigger (QK), who claims PP and two other black teenage males robbed and stabbed him. PP is indicted for Attempted Murder-1 and Robbery-1. QK has become something of a celebrity since the incident. Locally admired for fighting back, he has also been on local radio shows and at least one national television talk show.

Anytown is a typical middle-American city of about 500,000 people, of whom 85 percent are white, 10 percent are African American, and 5 percent are Hispanic. Juries in Anytown are usually all white, although occasionally one minority member will end up making the cut.

Prosecution Scenario

QK is a twenty-seven-year-old Caucasian resident of Anytown and is married to a stay-at-home wife. They have a two-year-old child and another one on the way. On Friday, May 6, 2011, QK was working alone in his clothing store, Quarrel's Cool Clothes, located on Fourth Avenue.[2] At about 12:45 p.m., QK says two black teenage males entered his establishment and began browsing through the racks. QK later told the 911 operator that "one of the boys was older, light skinned, tall, and had a long scar running down the right side of his face; the other was young, dark skinned, short, and had a distinctive blond goatee."

Shortly thereafter, QK says a third male entered the store, browsing. QK described this person, on the 911 call he made after the shooting, as slender but well built, height and age unknown, dark skinned, close-cropped hair, and wearing an orange sweater under a buttoned-up red-and-black-plaid lumberjack shirt or jacket, with a gold stud in his left ear and "TYC Members Only" tattooed on the back of his left hand. This third person asked QK

2. See the diagram on page 11.

about a brand of jeans Quarrel's Cool Clothes did not carry; then he left, with the first two young men following on his heels.

According to QK, about ten minutes later, at 1:00 p.m., the same three teens returned to, and entered, the store. The first two subjects remained near the door, with "Blondie" staring back into the store and "Scarface" watching the street. The third guy came to the counter and asked to see the best baggy jeans QK had, while at the same time displaying a thick roll of cash with a $20 bill on top.

Trying to keep all three in sight, QK says he showed the third guy to the back rack in the store. The third guy requested a certain size, and QK turned to a nearby shelf. Suddenly, he felt sharp stabbing pains in his back and fell to the floor. QK says he looked up and saw the third guy holding a steak knife. The third guy and "Blondie," who had come into the store, grabbed twelve of the most expensive jeans and ran out.

Once he heard the door slam, QK got up, got his .357 Magnum revolver from under the counter, and gave chase. Seeing a "a flash that looked kinda like red plaid" turning north into a crowd at the corner of Fourth and E, QK says he ran to the corner and saw the man who stabbed him running away about fifty feet up E Street. QK fired one shot. At first, and in every statement until the grand jury, QK claims he doesn't know if he hit the guy. At grand jury, he admits he shot PP "square in the back," saw him fall and lie still, and thought, *"Good, I killed the m-----f-----."* QK says he immediately returned to his store and called 911. On the 911 call, in every statement, in grand jury, and at trial, QK insists that he did not approach the body of the man he shot. QK gave the detailed descriptions mentioned above on the 911 call and said he fired from the E Street corner at the robber fifty feet north of Fourth Avenue.

Officer Krupke is the first officer to find PP lying facedown on E Street, 110 feet north of Fourth Avenue.

Krupke asks, "What happened?"

PP replies, "Don't know. Walking home . . . guy ran . . . by . . . got shot."

Krupke asks, "How do you feel?"

PP replies, "Am I dying? Feel's like I'm dying."

Officer Krupke observes PP as he stands over him and writes in his notebook that PP is "slender, well built, height and age unknown, close-cropped hair, and wearing an orange sweater under a buttoned-up red/black plaid lumberjack shirt/jacket, with a gold stud in his left ear, and 'TYC Members Only' tattooed on the back of his left hand." PP's head is cocked, such that the right side of his face is down on the pavement. His left hand is to the left of his left shoulder, palm down, and the right hand to the right of his right shoulder, palm up. Both legs are bent at the hip and the knee. There is no blood trail, only blood at the body. Officer Krupke recovers an expended large-caliber slug on the sidewalk ten feet south of the body.

Three days later, Officer Krupke shows QK a photo array containing five DMV photos. PP's photo is the first picture in the array, and PP clearly has the darkest complexion of anyone of the five shown. QK immediately picks PP's photo as the third robber, the stabber, and the man he chased and shot at. Officer Krupke pats QK on the back and says—"Good job. That's the guy."

Three weeks later, a lineup is held. PP is the only person in the lineup whose picture was also in the prior array. PP has noticeably darker skin than the others in the line. QK emphatically identifies PP as the person who robbed and stabbed him. Officer Krupke pats QK on the back and nods approvingly at him. QK is very emotional on the 911 tape and at the lineup. QK is 100 percent sure of his identification and tells your investigator, "I'll never forget that face. I see it in my dreams."

Evidence in Addition to Preceding Statements

Other available evidence is described by category below.

Forensic Evidence and Missing Evidence

Officer Krupke finds a knife with a bloody tip on the counter of the clothing store. Subsequent tests reveal no useable fingerprints on the weapon. Serology and DNA tests confirm that the blood on the knife is Quarrel's. Ballistics testing confirms that the slug found ten feet south of PP's body was fired from QK's .357 Magnum revolver.

Neither stolen baggy jeans nor any big roll of bills are recovered on or near PP, or at the store or shooting scenes, or anywhere else. Neither side finds any witnesses who saw any African American teenage males come running out of the store. Nor does anyone admit seeing QK run out with, and ultimately fire, his gun. Nor does anyone say they saw what happened after the shot, until police arrived.

Medical Evidence

Fortunately, QK's injuries were superficial—four stab wounds penetrating the skin less than a quarter-inch each. By contrast, PP suffered a through-and-through gunshot wound of the abdomen, consistent with being caused by a large-caliber handgun, like a .357 Magnum. The surgeon, Dr. Kildare, identifies the entrance wound as in front, about one inch above the navel and slightly left of the midline. Dr. Kildare finds the exit wound on PP's back, level with the entrance wound, but five inches left of the midline.

The records show low levels of cocaine in PP's system, indicating use sometime in the preceding ninety-six hours. The records also detail the multiple surgeries and heroic medical procedures required to save PP's life during his two-week stay in the hospital, before he was carted off to jail to await trial.

Tangible Evidence

The state seized PP's clothing from the hospital. Because it is obvious he suffered a gunshot wound, the state did not request lab analysis. We examine the clothing at the police department. Obvious bullet holes appear in the left back side of the orange sweater and the lumberjack shirt. These holes line up with each other, about five inches left of the midline and one inch above a line level with the navel. There are no other bullet holes in the clothing. There is a soaking bloodstain on the inside front of the orange sweater, just above where the wearer's navel would be.

Eleventh-Hour Surprise

Two weeks before trial, the cops bust fourteen-year-old Sucha Snitch (SS) on drug charges (four crack sales to undercover cops in the high school parking lot). He is short, dark skinned, and has a struggling blond goatee. SS is already on juvenile probation for armed robbery (purse theft from a teacher at knifepoint; unidentified African American accomplice-lookout was older, tall, light skinned, and had a long scar running down the right side of his face).

At the beginning of his statement to Officer Krupke, SS asks: "Am I being busted for stabbing that clerk on Fourth Avenue? Those damn pants didn't fit anyhow; I should have killed the m-----f-----!" Asked how many times he stabbed the clerk, SS says, "More than three and less than five, man." SS makes no mention of PP or anyone else participating with him in the Fourth Avenue robbery. Asked about accomplices, he replies: "Not saying. Not saying." SS denies associating with anyone named "Peter." Officer Krupke concludes that SS is the "Blondie" subject that QK described.

Officer Krupke contacts the DA, who promptly cuts a deal with SS's lawyer: no probation revocation on the prior armed-robbery case; a no-contest plea and delinquency adjudication with probation for simple possession of cocaine; all other pending crack-sale charges dismissed; no prosecution for the clothing store Attempted Murder-1/Robbery-1. All SS has to do is testify "truthfully." Under the deal, SS will remain in custody at TYC until after he testifies, at which point an expedited disposition hearing will be held so he can be released on probation.

By doing the deal with SS, the DA hopes to clinch the case against PP, who is already indicted in adult court and whom QK has already identified as the stabber. Contrary to every episode of *Law & Order,* police and prosecutors almost always prefer the first bird in their hand to having to reopen and rethink cases once they have filed charges.

Naturally, by the time he testifies at trial, SS will put the knife in PP's hand and identify him as the mastermind of the robbery. SS will also testify that he was PP's only accomplice, that QK was the only other person in the store, and that no scar-faced person was in the store or involved in the robbery and stabbing.

Diagram of the Scene of Events

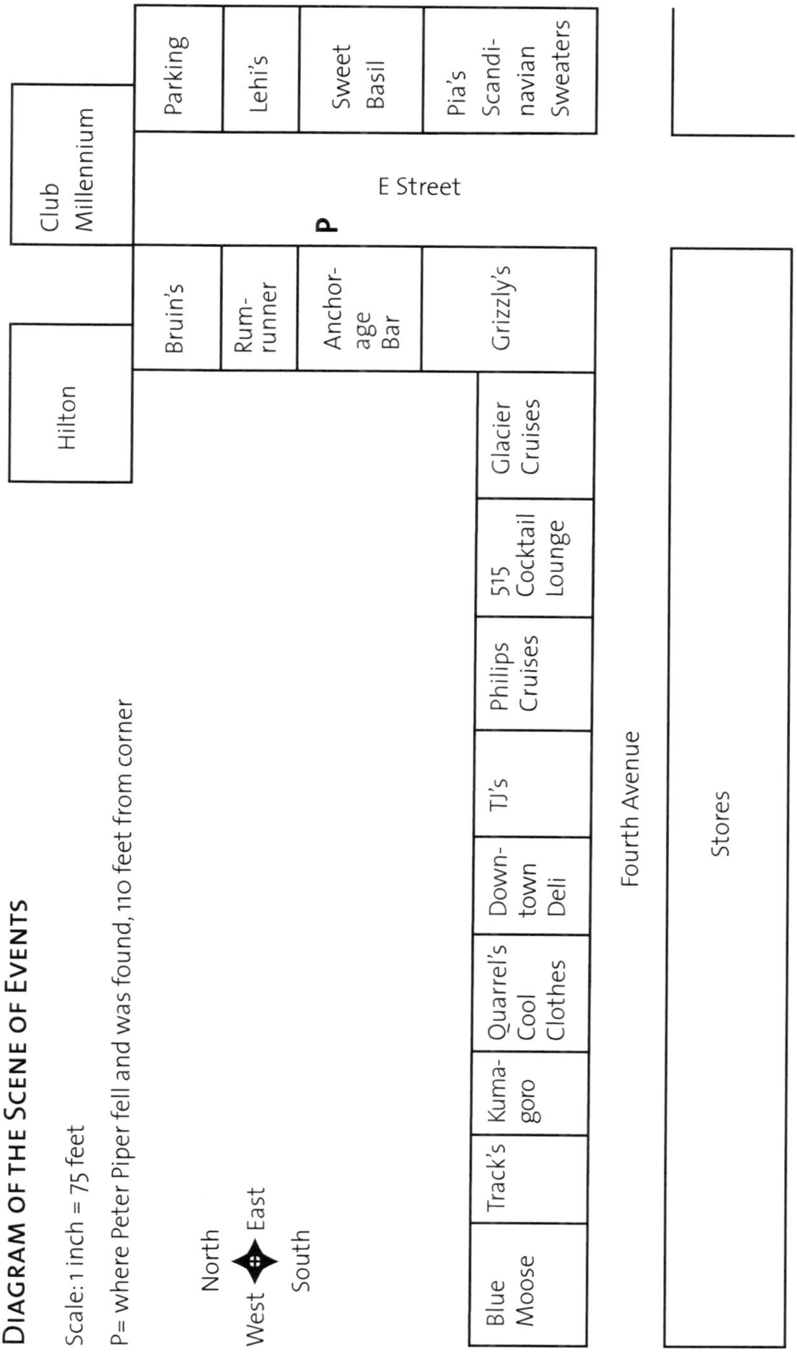

2

Determine the Outcome

Step One: Identify Legal and Factual Theories

Here, in place of a factually detailed case theory, we only identify the wide range of possible defenses in the case. (We will develop the factually detailed case theory in steps three and four of this chapter and in chapter 3, after we discuss what determines outcomes.) We list all broad theory strokes, because deciding what does or does not determine outcomes varies from case theory to case theory. For example, a theory of provocation by the complainant may be critical to a self-defense justification, but only interesting to an alibi claim.

The possible defenses in *Piper* include:

1. Insanity, diminished capacity, or voluntary intoxication

2. Duress

3. Self-defense or defense of others

4. QK's honest mistake of identification
5. Fabrication:
   - QK knows he shot an innocent bystander.
   - There was no robbery at all—maybe a drug deal or gambling-debt collection or an effort to hire arsonists.
   - QK may have stabbed himself and SS is lying to get his deal.
   - PP was never there, and SS is lying to get his deal.
6. Other suspects: SS and/or Scarface did it.

Sometimes defense theories are more legal than factual in nature. For instance, the kidnapping count in a rape-kidnapping case could turn on the issue of whether or not the degree of forcible movement of the complainant was sufficiently separate from the rape to constitute an additional offense. At the beginning, always review the statutes, case law, and jury instructions, which define potentially required elements and available defenses.

Use caution, because statutes often leave out legally required elements of the offense, such as *mens rea*[1] as to circumstance. Similarly, "pattern" jury instructions may omit or misstate essential elements. Case law is critical to gaining reliable knowledge of the elements of offenses and defenses. And, like Case Analysis, mastering the controlling case law is free; we just have to keep up with newly decided appellate opinions and research issues about which we are not certain.

Step Two: Identify *Outcome Levers*

The second step in this analysis asks the question: "What are the outcome levers in this case?" An outcome lever is anything—a fact,

1. The categories of criminal *mens rea* are commonly known to include intent, knowledge, recklessness, or criminal negligence.

a piece of evidence, a psychological reality, a jury feeling, a current event, a cultural phenomenon, or other factor—that is capable, in and of itself, of determining the outcome for one side or the other.

We must think broadly about any factors beyond the evidence that may determine the outcome. Even though legally irrelevant, such factors often control the result if we do not identify and deal with them effectively.

For example, in *Piper,* stereotypical thinking about race is a huge—though legally irrelevant—factor. An alleged crime by a group of black teens against a white shopkeeper triggers a lot of media- and culture-generated assumptions and beliefs about what probably happened. Some jurors may determine who's right and who's wrong in this case regardless of any evidence and notwithstanding the legal principles of presumed innocence or proof beyond a reasonable doubt. Accordingly, the shorthand term "race bias" tops the prosecution's list of outcome levers, even though it has little to do with the evidence and has no legal relevance. See the Outcome Levers diagram and discussion on the following pages.

In this case, other nonevidentiary outcome levers include P-4 and D-4, discussed in the following pages.

Sometimes outcome levers respond directly to each other; that is, one on one side is substantively answered by one on the other, and vice versa. In our example, SS testifying that PP participated in the crime with him and did the stabbing is an outcome lever for the state, but SS's admission to Officer Krupke that he was the stabber is an outcome lever for the defense.

On the next page is a list of the outcome levers for both sides in the *Piper* case. The use of a T-square separates the respective sides. Additionally, points that may directly respond to each other are juxtaposed across the centerline, while points that do not are staggered. We repeat this simple process throughout the case, as new information, new understanding, new analysis, and new rulings from the court affect our Case Analysis. We may develop half a dozen or more outcome lever T-squares by the end of the trial of a big case.

Outcome Levers: **State v. Peter Piper**

Prosecution	***Defense***
P-1: Race bias against PP • PP's priors • TYC incarceration • cocaine use	
	D-1: QK's huge reasons to lie
P-2: QK's positive eyewitness ID and detailed description of PP	D-2: QK's huge lies • QK is lying about knowing he shot PP. • QK is lying about the number of robbers. • QK is lying about going to PP's body.
	D-3: Physical evidence refutes QK.
P-3: No coincidence—all three suspects know one another, all are in a half-block radius at the same time, and one was shot due to the other two.	
P-4: Innocent victim stabbed	D-4: Anyone could be an innocent bystander, and PP has suffered enough. QK's wounds are superficial.
P-5: SS says he did it with PP.	D-5: SS is the stabber and did it with Scarface.
P-6: PP's testimony/failure to testify	D-6: PP's testimony/failure to testify

Prosecution Outcome Levers

The prosecution has six outcome levers, which will be presented in this section.

The P-1 Lever: Race Bias

The P-1 outcome lever, race bias, rests on cultural stereotypes—assumptions—that African American teenage males will act violently. Social psychology research overwhelmingly shows many white and black Americans share these attitudes.[2] Before the trial begins, the accused's and complainant's races generate forces that can themselves produce a conviction that otherwise might not occur if the verdict were based solely on the admissible evidence.

Such injustice can result from the jury's functionally lowering the "reasonable doubt" standard, reversing the presumption of innocence, or both. Racial stereotyping certainly provides a biased lens through which the jury will see the testimony and other evidence in the light most favorable to the state, and most harmful to the accused.

References to, or evidence about, the accused's prior record and incarceration at TYC for violent delinquency offenses, or current cocaine use, fit into this same point. Hostile jurors see these references as validating their preexisting attitudes.

The P-2 Lever: Eyewitness ID

The P-2 outcome lever is QK's emphatic and positive eyewitness identification of PP as the man who stabbed and robbed him. In reality, these kinds of identifications can often be unreliable. However, juries show little interest in challenges to the ability of innocent victims to identify their offenders. One big reason may be that positive identification relieves jurors of a lot of the responsibility for the verdict. The witness was there, and "knows" who hurt him. QK's prompt, detailed, repeated, and accurate description of PP also goes a long way to supporting this presumptive faith in identification testimony.

The P-3 Lever: No Coincidence

P-3 is the no-coincidence outcome lever. It relies on the implausibility that three teenage males who know one another (PP, SS, and Scarface) could all be within a block of one another at the exact same time, with one ending up shot, solely because of the independent and unknown activities of the other two. The degree of implausibility increases as the population size of the locale increases.

2. For more information, see appendices B and C.

The P-4 Lever: Empathy or Outrage

The P-4 lever, an innocent victim is stabbed, is the empathy or outrage outcome lever. Jurors are more likely to identify with the hardworking shopkeeper who is just trying to support his family than with the young marauders trying to rob and stab him just to get free jeans. Racial stereotyping exacerbates this dynamic, as discussed previously in the P-1 outcome lever. And where, unlike here, the complainant's injuries are fatal or life threatening, the horror of the crime itself is often an outcome lever for the state.

The P-5 Lever: Participant Evidence

The P-5 lever, SS says he did it with PP, is an evidentiary outcome lever. However sweet SS's deal—and however awful his own criminality—SS knows what happened in the store, because he admits he was there and was involved. If there is some corroboration from another source, such as QK's account, the jury only has to decide that SS is truthfully identifying his accomplice in order to convict. Because accomplices invariably know each other, much of the dirt flung at them tends to rebound to our clients, who are in some way associated with the accomplices.

The P-6 Lever: Our Client's Testimony

The P-6 lever, our client's testimony, is nearly always an outcome lever for both sides, which is why it is paired with D-6. If he testifies, Mr. Piper is capable, by himself, of winning the case, losing the case, or leaving doubt as to the correct verdict. All of these results can determine the outcome. Our client's *failure* to testify may or may not be an outcome lever for the state, depending on the individual facts and circumstances of the case.

Defense Outcome Levers

The defense also has six outcome levers it can use. These are detailed below.

The D-1 Lever: Kwiktrigger's Reasons to Lie

The D-1 lever, QK's huge reasons to lie, is the outcome lever that provides the foundation for a successful defense. Assuming PP is innocent, we are still unlikely to prevail by calling this an honest mistake of identification. See the discussion in the prosecution's section of the P-2 lever. If QK knows his identification of PP is incorrect, and PP is not involved, the critical question becomes: "Why would a man like QK lie by identifying an innocent man?"

The only credible answer to this question is that QK lied because he knew he shot the *wrong* man. If he knew he shot an innocent bystander, QK had many big reasons to lie: avoiding criminal and civil liability, protecting his family's sole income stream and their ability to remain together, and protecting his own good name.

The D-2 Lever: Kwiktrigger's Lies

The D-2 lever, QK's lies, consists of QK's provable lies and his highly implausible claims. These show that his reasons to lie (discussed in D-1) became the basis for his actual lying. First, his grand jury testimony shows that he lied to the 911 operator and the police in several statements about whether he knew he hit someone. Second, the big discrepancy between SS and QK as to how many teens were involved in the robbery suggests that QK added a third person to the fracas after realizing he had shot a mere bystander. Regardless of SS's contrary claims, we know that SS's longtime partner in crime, Scarface, was present and involved—why else would QK have been able to describe him? Finally, a commonsense behavioral analysis makes it necessary that QK approached PP's fallen body—an act that he steadfastly denies—because to admit it would unravel his whole cover-up story.

As we'll see in chapter 3, the fact of a contradiction or lie is a small starting point. The payoff comes when we can plausibly explain *why* someone is lying.

The D-3 Lever: Physical Evidence

The D-3 lever involves the physical evidence of the shooting. The biggest apparent contradiction between QK's claims (he shot PP in the back) and the physical evidence is Dr. Kildare's opinion that PP was shot in the *front* of his body. The entrance wound is one inch above the navel. This is an enormous problem for QK's claim that he shot the stabber in the back as he fled. Hitting someone in the front at a distance of one hundred feet is much more plausible if that person is an innocent bystander in a crowd of other innocent bystanders, walking toward—rather than fleeing from—the pursuer.

Unfortunately for the defense, if we carefully examine the clothes PP was wearing, we see they disprove Dr. Kildare's opinion. No bullet penetrated the clothes in front. There is only a soaking bloodstain that lines up with the inside of the sweater where the bullet exited PP's body one inch above the navel. Bullet-penetration holes do exist on the clothing and line up perfectly with the wound in PP's back, five inches left of the midline. Apparently, the bullet dissipated in force as it passed through PP's body, and just fell out of his clothes.

Without the shot-in-the-front point, D-3 does not really qualify as an outcome lever, because it involves so many separate, small factual elements. The overall concept of a liar's story being contradicted by physical evidence is a theme, which, in this case, is better developed in the chapter 3 construction of a plausible, persuasive reality of innocence.

The D-4 Lever: Empathy or Outrage

The D-4 lever, anyone could be an innocent bystander and be shot, pairs with P-4, an innocent victim is stabbed, as the empathy or outrage outcome lever. While there will not be much immediate empathy by jurors with the accused, any one of them, or their children, could have been walking down the street in the middle of the day when an enraged shopkeeper loosed off a shot into a crowd. We're all innocent bystanders, every day. The disparity in injury also may provide an implicit basis for PP-has-suffered-enough feelings in some jurors.

The D-5 Lever: Participant Evidence

The D-5 lever, SS's confession to Officer Krupke, is a piece of evidence that provides the factual basis for a successful exculpatory theory of the case. It establishes SS as the stabber and implies the participation of his frequent accomplice, "Scarface." The D-5 lever is paired with P-5, SS says he did it with PP, because, depending on how they play out, the same subject matter can determine the outcome for either side.

The D-6 Lever: Our Client's Testimony

D-6, our client's testimony, is nearly always an outcome lever for both sides, which is why it is paired with P-6. If he testifies, PP is capable, by himself, of winning the case, losing the case, or leaving doubt as to the correct verdict. All of these results help determine the outcome.

Step Three: Maximize or Minimize Outcome Levers

Once we identify outcome levers on both sides, we must devise means to maximize the defense levers and eliminate or minimize the prosecution levers. This is where creativity in forging and effectively using new, powerful tools is at a premium. There are many ways of doing this. Some of the most readily available means include the following:

- Investigation
- Continuing Case Analysis
- Pretrial motions litigation
- Arranging expert testimony
- Preparing to cross-examine opposing witnesses
- Preparing defense witnesses to testify
- Preparing the accused's appearance and demeanor in court
- Preparing the accused to testify
- Juror investigation and questionnaires
- Voir dire
- Well-founded and timely objections

- Jury instructions
- Opening and closing argument

Minimizing P-1: Race Bias

Beginning with the racial stereotyping concern in P-1 (race bias), jury questionnaires and voir dire are critical to eliminating, or at least minimizing, this problem. Everyone has been stereotyped in some way in daily life, and approaching the issue from that perspective is often a productive lead-in for voir dire questions on this difficult subject.[3]

Other tools include cross-examining QK on his willingness to use deadly force and his expectation that people would believe him, because of race. Special jury instructions—like a race-switching instruction—can also be effective.[4] What is the argument against such a charge? Should the prosecution get the benefit of racial stereotyping in convicting the accused, even if the basis is impermissible and unconstitutional? We can also use opening and closing argument to reduce the negative effects of racial bias.

In some cases, we might want to use expert testimony from a research psychologist on the impact of racial stereotypes on witness perception, memory, and recounting.[5]

As for the part of P-1's dealing with PP's prior record, incarceration, and recent cocaine use, we must file motions *in limine,* or request protective orders, to exclude any such evidence and references.[6] If the judge denies the motions, then we will use voir dire, special jury instructions, and argument to minimize the harm. The ruling on the admissibility of such evidence will be a factor in the decision whether to call PP as a witness.

PP's incarceration at TYC seems to be the most likely to come in, in some form, since that is how SS claims to know him, and because the "TYC" tattoo is an important part of QK's description. Note, however, if our defense is that QK is lying instead of making an honest mistake, the tattoo proves less. While we can use euphemisms like

3. See appendix A for sample questions.
4. See appendix B.
5. See appendix C for notice of such an expert.
6. An example is provided in appendix D.

"residential school," if one juror knows what TYC means, speculation among the jurors will fuel prejudice that surpasses the effect of an honest statement and special limiting jury instruction.

Special—that is, nonpattern—jury instructions are the unmined gold of the trial process. While standard pattern instructions are often ineffective in curbing prejudice, special instructions are frequently effective. There are four components to an effective special limiting instruction:

1. Identify the only permissible uses of the evidence.
2. Identify the impermissible uses.
3. Explain to the jury why those latter uses are forbidden.
4. Use strong admonitory language.[7]

Minimizing P-2: Positive Identification

QK's positive identification of PP—the P-2 point—is only a problem if the defense theory is that QK is honestly mistaken. By changing the defense to deliberate fabrication of some of his story, as discussed in points D-1 and D-2 above, we neuter the otherwise-powerful eyewitness identification testimony. Of course, QK will vehemently identify PP, even at trial—that's a key part of QK's cover-up. That's also why we need to conduct a Dynamic Cross-Examination of QK to undermine QK's initially plausible story.[8] In this way, we can make two defense outcome levers defeat a key prosecution outcome lever.

Maximizing D-1 and D-2: QK Is Lying

We will hit the D-1 and D-2 points (QK's reasons to lie, and what QK's lies are) throughout the trial to maximize their impact. We'll start in voir dire by discussing what it would take to make a "good" man lie. Maybe he needed to make an immediate decision. Would that immediate need cause him to lie? Why might he think he'd get away with it (remember Susan Smith)? Why could this man not change his story later and tell the truth? We

7. See appendix E for examples.
8. *See Dynamic Cross-Examination*, *supra* chapter 1, note 1.

emphasize this critical defense position in our opening statement, cross-examination, defense case, and closing argument. We can even request special jury instructions on aspects of credibility such as bias, motive to lie, and interest in the outcome.

Minimizing P-3: Coincidences

We minimize the P-3 outcome lever—proximity, relationships, time, and intersecting events are no coincidence—at the macro and micro levels. The macro level includes investigating to find out how many people are typically in the downtown area in the middle of a business day at that time of year, and specifically the number of African Americans. We may be able to produce powerful visual evidence by making videotapes and taking pictures to show the congestion on Fourth Avenue at 12:45 to 1:00 p.m. on comparable afternoons close in time to the incident.

The micro answer also depends on investigation. In this case, the answer might be to determine and develop evidence that PP may know SS but does not associate with him. Scarface, not PP, is in SS's crew. Aiding this effort is the four-year age difference between PP and SS. Even if they knew each other from TYC, it should not be hard to show that they ran in very different circles.

Additionally, we can undermine the P-3 outcome lever (all three know one another and are in the same half block at the same time) by showing that the state's case relies on one or more claimed coincidences of even greater magnitude. Thus, the coincidence that the state asserts against the defense in P-3 pales in comparison to the coincidences SS wants the jury to swallow. SS's coincidences are that, although SS was involved in and caught for two armed robberies where Scarface stood lookout, there was no older, tall, light-skinned, and scar-faced teen who stood lookout in this robbery. We can use this stretch to minimize, by comparison, the point the prosecution makes in P-3.

Removing D-3: Physical Evidence

The D-3 outcome lever (hard physical evidence establishes the defense) drops out. Once the jury correctly understands that the gunshot wound goes from the left side of PP's back to the front, the remaining physical inconsistencies do not amount to an outcome lever. However, they will be important components of the plausible, persuasive reality constructed in chapter 3.

P-4 and D-4: Innocent Victim or Innocent Bystander?

In stressing the P-4 outcome lever (an innocent victim was stabbed), the state may try to elicit testimony from QK's wife, friends, church members, or other community members who know him. All of these witnesses are great fodder for cross-examination, establishing the desperate reliance that QK's family has on his ability to work. Such witnesses may help the D-1 motive theory (QK's reasons to lie) as much or more than the P-4 lever (an innocent victim is stabbed). Wouldn't a devoted family man and sole supporter do anything it took to protect his family—including falsely blaming a black teenage male, whom he had the poor judgment to shoot, and who appeared to be dead or dying anyway?

These witnesses are also ideal for establishing the D-4 point: anyone, including them, could be innocent bystanders. How many of them have been shopping on that very block? How about their friends? How many of their children have been in QK's shop, looking at jeans? Have they ever seen someone run 250 feet down the street and loose off a gun into a crowd? What would they have done? Why?

Medical testimony will establish the comparative severity of QK's and PP's injuries. However, jury nullification in favor of black teenage males is rare in cases that allege violent crimes against white complainants. The medical testimony will also lay the groundwork, so we can accurately reconstruct PP's position at the time of the shooting.

P-5 and D-5: Maximizing Our View of the Participant Evidence

We should handily win the P-5/D-5 pairing (SS says he did it with PP; means that SS was the stabber and did it with Scarface). We should win this not because SS got the deal of the century—all snitches are bought with huge inducements—yet most juries believe them for the reasons explained in the P-5 discussion. Here, we should win, because we can use SS's initial spontaneous confession to stabbing QK, along with his long-standing criminal association and activities with Scarface, to solve the crime without PP's being present or involved at all.

Of course, in real life, the most we are likely to find out about SS from the prosecution is that he cut a deal and the terms. We must immediately seek and obtain judicial orders to unseal the juvenile court proceedings and social file in SS's prior cases along with the change-of-plea hearing that was part of his deal. Once unsealed, we will immediately get copies of the documents and a tape and transcript of the hearing.

Once we know about SS's prior cases, move for Rule 17(c) subpoenas to the police for the reports, witness statements, and other documents created in his other cases. Given SS's claim that he got tight with PP at TYC, we also want to get all records from that institution about PP (by a consent form) and SS (by a 17(c) subpoena). In addition, we'll interview the people at TYC who had contact with PP and SS during the time of their overlap there to further show the absence of a relationship between them.

Only by doing these investigatory and preparatory tasks do we uncover the critical factual links between SS's prior theft, his prior knifepoint robbery of his teacher, and the present stabbing and robbery of QK. This is also the only way to prove that PP and SS had no contact and association at TYC. At the time, SS was twelve and PP was sixteen.

SS's motive to lie is not enough. Enumerating his lies is not enough. What *is* enough is showing a plausible reality in which his lies protect his true accomplice, Scarface, and himself, the actual stabber. The prosecution will fight hard to keep out the Scarface connection, so we must file a well-researched and well-reasoned motion *in limine* to introduce evidence of SS's and Scarface's prior criminal connections and activities.[9]

9. See appendix F.

P-6 and D-6: What to Do about Our Client's Testimony

Which way the P-6 and D-6 pairing, our client's testimony, will cut remains unknown. Will PP need to testify in the case? Will the risk of his priors, TYC incarceration, and cocaine use keep him off the stand? File motions! Once we prepare him effectively, will PP be a good witness? He really doesn't have much weight to carry in his story of walking down the street and being shot. On the other hand, the lack of important information that PP knew reduces the jury expectation that he should testify. A pre-trial motion to admit PP's excited utterance to Officer Krupke is important and, if granted, may further reduce the need for him to testify.

Generally speaking, the rule is that in a nonhomicide case, there must be a compelling reason for the accused to testify. On the other hand, in a homicide case, there must be a compelling reason for the accused *not* to testify. There are several reasons for this difference. The most important is that, in homicide cases, we can't cross-examine the complainant in court—he's dead. The *Piper* case is a perfect example: we will win or lose it when we cross-examine QK.

There is one caveat about the accused's testimony rule. Because this generation has *Law & Order* assumptions about guilt, the legal process, and the supposed characteristics of defendants, victims, prosecutors, and defense attorneys, the client's testimony is necessary in more cases than it would have been thirty years ago.

Step Four: Choose the Best Theory of the Case

Two major results of analyzing outcome levers greatly affect how we choose the best defense theory.

First, the lying and cover-up story is better for the defense than the honest mistaken-identity story. The lying and cover-up approach gives us fewer obstacles from the state's evidence and more opportunities to create evidence tending to show PP's innocence.

Second, SS's claim that this was a robbery, and that one of the robbers stabbed QK, eliminates a lot of other scenarios about what might have been happening in the store. SS's claim also eliminates the self-inflicted-wound idea. We must consciously decide whether to accept or reject SS's self-implication. In doing so, it seems clear that SS's spontaneous confession to stabbing QK in his talk with Officer Krupke is far more beneficial than speculating about other scenarios, which are not supported by much evidence.

Accordingly, the original list of possible defense theories now looks like this. The most likely defenses are in bold.

1. Insanity or Diminished Capacity
2. Duress
3. Self-Defense or Defense of Others
4. QK's Honest Mistake of Identification
5. **Fabrication: QK knows he shot an innocent bystander and is trying to cover it up.**
   - There was no robbery at all. It may have been a drug deal, a gambling-debt collection, or an effort to hire arsonists.
   - QK may have stabbed himself.
   - **SS is lying to get his deal, and PP was never there.**
   - SS is lying to get his deal, and he wasn't even there.
6. **Other Suspect: SS and Scarface did it.**

All of these three likely positions fit neatly into a single defense theory. Given that factual defense, we can revisit the outcome levers we identified previously and weight them. In light of the unified defense theory, the outcome levers for each side that will have the biggest effect on the case are shown in bold.

Weighted Outcome Levers: State v. Peter Piper

Prosecution	*Defense*
P-1: Race bias against PP **• PP's priors** **• TYC incarceration** **• cocaine use**	
	D-1: QK's huge reasons to lie
P-2: QK's positive eyewitness ID and detailed description of PP	**D-2: QK's huge lies** **• QK is lying about knowing he shot PP.** **• QK is lying about the number of robbers.** **• QK is lying about going to PP's body.**
	D-3: Physical evidence refutes QK.
P-3: No coincidence—all three suspects know one another, all are in a half-block radius at the same time, and one was shot due to the other two.	
P-4: Innocent victim stabbed	D-4: Anyone could be an innocent bystander, and PP has suffered enough. QK's wounds are superficial.
P-5: SS says he did it with PP.	**D-5: SS is the stabber and did it with Scarface.**
P-6: PP's testimony/failure to testify	D-6: PP's testimony/failure to testify

Step Five: Identify and Deal with Trapdoors

The final, but critical, step in this analysis is to ask: "What are the trapdoors in this case?"

A *trapdoor* is reasoning by which jurors can buy most of our position but still return a verdict against our client. It means we can win the battles and still lose the war.

The *Piper* case has two main trapdoors. The jury could agree that PP was not the stabber but decide that he was a participant in some other way in the robbery. Or the jury could agree that QK only got PP's description by approaching his body after shooting him and then lied about that, but that QK is right anyhow—it was PP who stabbed and robbed him.

Once we identify the trapdoors, we must develop strategies for keeping them shut.

The first trapdoor happens with some frequency. Lawyers trying cases often don't detect it, since criminal cases result in general verdicts. Although there is no evidence at all that PP played any role other than that of the principal—QK and SS both testify he was—jurors may still want to convict him for being somehow "involved." This desire can emanate from racial stereotyping (hostile to PP or sympathetic to QK), *Law & Order* assumptions, the derogatory impact of evidence of prior crimes or incarceration, the high community profile of the case, or any number of other factors.

The best way to keep this trapdoor shut is to get explicit instructions from the judge that the jury must find, beyond a reasonable doubt, that PP "personally and physically" robbed QK and "personally and physically" stabbed QK. This can easily go into the elements instruction and should not be controversial, because there is no evidence PP did anything else.[10]

Other tools we can use are: motions for judgment of acquittal on any aiding-and-abetting theory, and special jury-verdict forms that require factual findings instead of a general "guilty" or "not guilty" verdict.

We can batten the second trapdoor by fully developing PP's plausible, persuasive reality of innocence. In this reality, the only reason QK would lie about not approaching the body—when he actually did—is if he discovered by doing so that he shot an innocent bystander. In this case, he used the access of approaching to discover he shot the wrong man, and to make the detailed description he falsely claimed to have seen of PP in his store.[11]

10. See appendix G.
11. See chapter 3.

In addition to the methods discussed above, we can keep trapdoors shut by directly addressing them in the closing argument. We will explain to the jury that speculation, compromise, and invention are not permissible. We'll invoke their duty to decide the case solely on the evidence, lack of evidence, and legal rules that the court provides.

3

Develop the Facts—Create a Plausible, Persuasive Reality

The Seven Pillars of Our Factual Reality

There is always much more room in the facts of any case than most lawyers think there is. Our responsibility is to create our own reality of innocence out of the traditional facts and from the better facts we develop through Case Analysis, investigation, and trial preparation.

The reality we will offer to the jury must be:

- Productive. The reality must be capable of producing an acquittal. Usually this includes a legal path to verdict, like self-defense or alibi. A position the court finds to be legally insufficient will not get instruction support and is not likely to prevail with the jury in a major criminal trial. So we must determine—from the start—which elements and defenses will end up in the jury instructions. Only rarely in a case involving serious harm is the successful path created by nullification or some other nonlegal, factual basis for the verdict.

- Possible. The factual claims in our reality must be physically and conceptually possible. This often requires that we reenact, research, and consult experts during preparation. For instance, if our defense relies on PP's being shot in the front as he walked toward QK, based on Dr. Kildare's demonstrably impossible opinion on the location of the entrance wound, then our defense is in a lot of trouble.[1]

- Plausible. This is a critical requirement. The reality we sponsor does not need to be the only possible factual solution, but it must be one that makes intuitive sense to ordinary men and women. They have to have a "Yeah, I can see that happening" reaction.

- Persuasive. Once we identify a plausible reality, we have to relentlessly build onto it. We move it from being intuitively plausible to truly persuasive. We must combine rigorous factual development and creative emotional and logical appeals. Then we connect the jurors' duty to the desired outcome, in order to accomplish this persuasive result.

- Playable. The reality cannot be too close factually to the conviction that the opponent seeks. If it is, we can score an own-goal or safety (pick your sport). We must move our factual reality a little farther away. By doing so, we avoid the own-goal risk and still leave room for the jury to choose the position of innocence that is too close to jeopardy if they want to do so.

  For example, a defense that PP was innocently present in the store—earlier that day or at the time of the robbery—and QK is confused or honestly transferring that memory to one of the actual robbers puts us way too close to conviction. With this additional concession, the P-3 no-coincidence outcome lever will bury this defense. If a juror

1. See D-3 in the previous chapter.

or two wants to acquit on the transference basis, great; they can go there on their own. It's just not something we can effectively advocate.

- Powerful. Our plausible, persuasive reality has to move the jury to act, whether from empathy, emotion, logic, or duty—or, most likely, a combination of all of these. We must create dynamics in the courtroom sufficient to cause the jurors to do something they are often very reluctant to do. Our utterly sincere communication throughout the trial, the power of our message, the power of our presentation, and the power of their responsibility, will, in the end, move jurors to do those remarkable things we know they are capable of doing.
- Provable. When the reality we offer is plausible and persuasive, it doesn't take much in the way of "proof" to make it work. A trial is a long, sometimes complicated, communication; it's not a science lab. And once we have a plausible, persuasive reality going, it is constantly amazing how preexisting "facts" fit, or can now be interpreted to fit, into that reality of innocence.

General Considerations about "Facts" in Any Case

The given facts are the beginning, not the end. Far too often, we think of the facts of a case like we did in law school. The appellate opinions we studied there presented the "facts" as if they were absolute, and limited. Professors called on students to "state the facts of the case," as if they are an immutable, finite entity that they can read and learn. Of course, in the real world of trial-level litigation, this doesn't happen. Very few facts are immutable, the number of facts is nearly infinite, and we cannot learn the facts just by reading about them in the discovery provided by our opponent.

One of the horrible side effects of "open file" discovery in criminal cases is that so many defense attorneys tend to take the often-voluminous, police-generated reports and witness interviews as the "facts of the case." It was a great experience to begin my practice in a jurisdiction like Washington, DC, Superior Court, where discovery was minimal. I learned to combine independent defense investigation, extensive motions practice, and creative Case Analysis to produce defenses far more effective than anything I could glean solely from information the police provided. I learned that the plausible, persuasive reality of innocence is not just made up of traditional facts.

There are always a few hard facts—like the date and some scientifically determined claims, although we can often successfully dispute them too. But soft facts such as witness observations—visual, auditory, tactile, olfactory, tasting, and the not-always-so-permissible inferences witnesses draw from them—are more common by far.

Both the hard- and soft-fact categories also include *absence of facts:* the nonexistence of an event, observation, or condition that we might expect to be associated with the fact. Paying acute attention to these absences is the first, and easiest, way to substantially expand the field of relevant "facts."

All facts and opinions that lay or expert witnesses testify to depend on the credibility of the witnesses who perceive, remember, and report them. The police typically ignore this reality in their investigations and in the witness statements they take. What happened? is the focus, not How believable is this witness? or Why would things go down that way?

By far the most effective attack on credibility is not general or peripheral. Instead, credibility attacks are much more powerful when they reveal bias; motive to lie; indifference to the truth; other interests in the litigation, participants, or outcome; or a prior pattern of relevant behavior or dishonesty. Legally, such bias, motive, and interest credibility attacks are much harder for the prosecutor to prevent or curtail, because they lie at the heart of the state and federal constitutional rights to due process and confrontation.

Once we take the impact of a good bias, motive, and interest attack into account, it is apparent that facts in the trial process bear almost no resemblance to the facts in law school—or for that matter the facts in discovery. Credibility issues swing the door wide to creative deconstruction and completely different factual realities. For example, when SS testifies that he saw PP stab QK, if the jury disbelieves that testimony, it may not only erase a damning fact against PP but may also result in the jury's finding new, inferred facts—that SS himself was the stabber, and that he lied about PP in order to cover up his own criminal activity.

In general, witnesses's and jurors' abilities to find facts plausible and persuasive is influenced by their:

- Preexisting beliefs and attitudes about the subject
- Implications and speculations beyond the facts
- Assumptions about how things work in their world and the worlds around them
- Assumptions about likely human behavior, including racial, gender, and sexual-orientation stereotypes
- Perceived public, community, family, or friends' attention, opinions, and feelings
- Dominating religious, moral, or political beliefs or agendas
- Personal value systems

The Interdependence of Facts

Credibility aside, in analyzing a witness's assertion of facts, we must realize that any fact—if *true*—logically and necessarily:

- Means some other facts must also be true.
- Means some other facts cannot be true.
- May or may not affect other facts in the case.

For example: if it is *true* that QK never approached PP's body, then he could not have gotten his detailed description from personally observing PP shot and fallen on the ground. It may also be true he did not know at the scene whether or not he shot the right person. It may well support his claim that his opportunity to observe PP's person, face, and clothes in detail occurred in his store, during the robbery and stabbing, before any chase and shooting.

Conversely, and credibility aside, a fact—if *false*—logically and necessarily:

- Means some other facts must also be false.
- Means some other facts must be true.
- May or may not affect other facts in the case.

For example, if it is *false* that QK never approached PP's body, then it is true that QK *did* approach PP's body. And it is true that QK could observe the details of PP's description as he lay shot and fallen on the ground. It may also be true that, when QK saw who he shot at close range, he immediately knew it was not the robber-stabber. Thus, it may also be true that QK used the face and appearance he observed standing over PP in order to insert PP into the robbery-stabbing scenario and to cover up QK's own grievous mistake.

We Develop the Facts to Create a Plausible, Persuasive Reality of Innocence

The cornerstone of our plausible, persuasive reality of innocence in this case is the fact that QK lied when he denied approaching PP's fallen body after shooting him. In our reality, QK did approach PP on the ground and did examine the person he shot—realizing, to his horror, that he hit an innocent bystander, not one of the robbers. In this way, we explain how QK knew PP's face and detailed description, even though PP was never in the store—it came from QK seeing PP fallen on the ground.

Establishing QK's lie begins with analyzing plausible human behavior in the circumstances as they arose. This looks at not only what QK claims he did, but also what he didn't do, and compares his conduct to what we think the jury would reasonably expect someone in his situation would do. The first point is that QK does not simply lock his store and call 911 after the attack. He could have created a place of safety for himself in the store and immediately gotten the authorities involved. Instead, he got up, went to the counter, grabbed his gun, and left the store—without locking it—in order to do what?

By the time he got to the door, at most he claimed to see "a flash that looked kinda like red plaid," all the way up at Fourth Avenue and E Street. He didn't see any other possible robbers. The diagram (see page 11) shows that the easiest and best escape route for the robbers would have been to turn west out of the store, run the short part of Fourth Avenue (about one hundred feet), and disappear around the corner into the road construction on F Street. This is a plausible reality we will offer the jurors: *that two actual robbers—SS and Scarface—were gone in the opposite direction, before QK even got out the door.*

By QK's account, having seen the flash of plaid at Fourth Avenue and E Street, he ran more than 250 feet, almost the length of a football field. In this same time, QK claimed, PP only covered fifty feet north on E Street, which is where QK saw and shot him. In other words, QK ran a distance five times longer than PP ran in the same amount of time. This huge implausibility strongly supports the inference that the real robbers were long gone and that PP was just an innocent bystander.

In any event, QK left a place of safety, abandoned his store, ran more than 250 feet with his big gun and superficial (but bleeding) injuries, turned the corner, and fired off a round. He said he was aiming at someone fifty feet away, but he hit PP, who was one hundred feet away. PP then stumbled another ten feet and fell to the ground.

Plausible reality tells us that QK knew perfectly well, after all of that effort directed at shooting someone, whether or not he hit anyone. And yet, this is the first lie QK told. Repeatedly, on the 911 call and in all his police interviews, QK claimed not to know if he hit anyone. Finally, in grand jury, he admitted he knew all the time that he hit someone. Then QK added, rather grandiosely, that he thought at the time, *"Good, I killed the m-----f-----."*

We must analyze this now-admitted first series of lies. Why in the world would QK admit to chasing PP and shooting his gun, then lie about whether he knew he hit someone and dropped him on the street? If he knew he hit the robber-stabber, he has no reason to lie. He would take credit—"Yeah, I shot the guy who stabbed me. You can collect him on E Street." Conversely, if QK knew he hit an innocent bystander, it is much more plausible that he would lie about knowing that his shot took effect. And so, even this initial lie becomes strong proof in support of our plausible, persuasive reality of innocence.

QK knew he shot an innocent man, and he tried to cover it up as best he could from the start. That he admitted this smaller, undeniable lie in the grand jury does not deprive it of impact. By the time of grand jury, QK's decision to save himself by falsely blaming PP is well on the way to achievement.

Now let's go back to the corner and examine a bigger lie. QK left safety, abandoned his store, and ran more than 250 feet after the "flash" he hoped was the robber-stabber. He felt the blood on his back from the stab wounds, he was really angry, he turned the corner, he fired his big gun, and he saw PP stagger and fall. What is his next plausible move? Turn around and go back to the store?

Hardly. All of the movement and momentum was east to and north up E Street. If he shot the robber, QK should be able to recover hundreds of dollars' worth of stolen pants lying there next to the fallen man. For all he knew, he might have only winged the man, who might get up or crawl away and escape if QK left him. How bad was he shot? Did he need an ambulance? The whole impetus of chasing and shooting one's quarry is to go up to it and examine what one has just shot.

In our plausible, persuasive reality, that is exactly what QK did. Holding his .357 out in front of him, in case the "robber" tried to flee again, QK approached the fallen man he shot. There were no jeans near the man, and he saw that the man on the ground was not one of the teens who had been in his store. Standing there, stomach falling, throat tightening, sweat running, QK started thinking about what was going to happen to him for shooting, maybe killing, an innocent bystander.

QK only had a few moments to decide what to do. He could call in and be honest with the police—then suffer a criminal prosecution for at least attempted murder and a civil lawsuit that could cost his family its sole means of support and ruin his reputation. Or he could just add PP into the robbery story. Just take the description of the man lying on the ground and make him the stabber. Then instead of two robbers—Blondie and Scarface—doing the attack, there are three—those two and the man he shot. So QK slipped the gun under his shirt, went back to his store, called 911, and lied to begin the cover-up.

Does QK really think he can get away with these lies? First, it doesn't matter, because, from his perspective, he has no other choice. Second, QK has a good chance of pulling this off. If PP is dead or dies, he will not be around to assert his noninvolvement. Even if he lives and is charged, who will an Anytown jury believe—the white shopkeeper who was robbed and stabbed by someone or the eighteen-year-old black male with TYC tattooed on his hand? Moreover, if caught and charged, SS will be delighted that PP is being blamed for SS's own stabbing. Neither SS nor Scarface will gain anything by insisting that one of them was the stabber.

In addition to expectations of plausible human behavior, more evidence supports the conclusion that QK went up to PP's body. Although otherwise detailed in every way, QK's description of PP includes "height and age unknown." How is that possible? QK gave both SS's and Scarface's comparative height estimates. According to QK, PP was not only in the store with those two, but was face-to-face with QK, discussing jeans, twice. The easiest, most automatic perception is whether someone you are talking to face-to-face is shorter, taller, or the same height as you. On the other hand, if the only time QK saw PP was after shooting him, as he lay on the ground with his legs bent, then it is likely QK wouldn't know PP's height.

More evidence supports this point. Officer Krupke, who only ever saw PP while standing over him on E Street, wrote down the identical description QK gave, including "height unknown." In our reality, QK and Officer Krupke had the identical view of PP—standing over him after he was shot and fallen, where everything about him and his clothes was easily visible, except his height and age.

Other facts tend to support our reality of PP's innocence and establish that QK approached the fallen PP. No roll of bills, with or without a $20 bill on the outside, was found between the store and where PP lay, nor was any recovered from PP's person. No stolen jeans were found between the store and where PP lay, nor were any recovered from PP's person. No fingerprints of PP's were found on the knife or anything else in the store. Other than QK and SS, no witnesses claim they saw PP in the store, running out of the store east on Fourth Avenue, or running north on E Street.

PP's spontaneous utterance also points toward his innocence. When Officer Krupke asked, "What happened?" PP replied, "Don't know. Walking home . . . guy ran . . . by . . . got shot . . . Am I dying? Feel's like I'm dying." This simple statement is PP's direct assertion that he was an innocent bystander to whatever was going on.

The medical testimony corroborates PP's statement and contradicts QK's grand jury testimony. QK claims he shot the fleeing stabber "square in the back." By contrast, the medical evidence shows that PP was more sideways to the weapon's barrel at the time he was shot. Maybe PP was turning to look at the guy running past, or maybe he was trying to turn away from the gun QK was pointing down the block. Both are consistent with an entry wound on the back side five inches left of the midline leading in a straight line to an exit wound in front, one inch above the navel.

Finally, the *why* of QK's lie about not approaching the body proves he was aware that he shot an innocent man. Only if he knew that he shot an innocent man would QK have any reason to lie about approaching the body. If he saw that he shot the robber-stabber, he would have no reason to deny examining the body. QK's repeated insistence on his wholly implausible claim—that he never went up to the body—strongly suggests that he *did.* That was how he learned he made a terrible mistake, which had the potential to ruin his own life and the life of the innocent bystander, who lay still on the sidewalk. No wonder PP's face is the one QK will never forget, the one he sees in his dreams. It is the face he saw after shooting and running up to a fallen, innocent man. This is why this single lie by QK is an outcome lever, which, alone, can produce an acquittal.

A great advantage of this reality is that we do not need to vilify QK as evil incarnate in front of an Anytown jury. After all, someone did rob and stab him. His mistakes in shooting wildly, lying, and covering up when he saw he hit the wrong man are grave, but understandable. How many people do we know, who, after having been robbed and stabbed, then shooting the wrong man, would actually tell the truth about it? Few, if any. We can understand why he concocted lies in the very few minutes he had to put them in play—all to save himself and his family.

But we sure won't let those lies send an innocent man to prison because of the crisis QK created by running down the street and shooting the wrong man. This part of the reality—based on a broad human understanding of the events—will be highly palatable to jurors.

Sucha Snitch in the Reality of PP's Innocence

The late arrival of SS on the prosecution scene is a huge blessing in disguise to the defense. True, most snitch cases result in conviction, because the defense attacks are general and fail to take seriously the risk of having an admitted participant point the finger of guilt—"him, too"—at our client. But in this case, our Case Analysis develops a plausible, persuasive reality, which not only absorbs SS, but affirmatively uses him to show PP's innocence in several ways.

First, once arrested, SS spontaneously confessed to Officer Krupke that he was the stabber in the QK attack. This is not a typical confession to the police—no interrogation or pressure—it's more like SS expected this day to come and assumed the police finally came to get him for the QK attack. In most jurisdictions, this confession is substantive evidence of the truth of its content.

In other jurisdictions, the due process clause should give it the same legal effect. In any event, the jury will understand it as the truth when we fit it into the overall defense reality.

Details in the content of SS's confession help to increase its impact. SS's specific references include: he wanted to kill QK, the stolen jeans didn't fit, he accurately knew the number of stab wounds, and he denied associating with anyone named Peter. These references establish elements of the crimes against SS and exculpate PP for the precise conduct QK alleges against him.

The second useful area to develop is SS's prior criminality with Scarface. This is important, but not to show SS is a violent gangbanger. Instead, proving that SS previously committed a robbery against his teacher, using a knife, corroborates SS's confession to Krupke. Even more important is that the teacher robbery involved two perpetrators—SS as the principal with the knife and his lookout, an older, tall African American, light-skinned teenage male, with a long scar running down the right side of his face.

If we take these facts and develop them together, they solve the crimes charged against PP—SS and Scarface did the QK robbery and stabbing. We know SS and Scarface were in the store and involved in the robbery—SS admits he was, and how else could QK possibly have described Scarface? SS insists in his trial testimony that only two people (now he says him and PP) were in the robbery. So parts of the truth are slipping out of both QK and SS. There were two robbers—SS and his demonstrated partner in crime, Scarface. This development also explains why QK had to add PP to the story, after finding out that he shot the wrong man. Suddenly, QK needed three robbers.

Getting the details of the teacher robbery admitted as evidence will be difficult if the admission theory is limited to a prior bad act to impugn the general credibility of SS. But once we develop the reality of PP's innocence to show how the evidence supports the conclusion that only SS and Scarface were involved, the likelihood of admission rises exponentially. SS's prior knifepoint robbery is unquestionably reliable evidence. It goes to the heart of the defense, and it will be admitted on evidentiary and constitutional bases.[2]

2. See appendix F.

Third, we investigate, prepare, and present evidence that PP was never a friend or associate of SS. Given the four-year age difference, this is not too hard to establish. We investigate for evidence, both in the community and at TYC, that shows they associated with different people and that there was never any trust-requiring relationship between them. The better the evidence of lack of contact, the stronger the reason to doubt PP would undertake a risky daylight violent crime with these perpetrators. Not only does this evidence corroborate SS's original confession—he associated with no one named Peter—but it also strengthens the idea that SS and Scarface alone robbed and stabbed QK.

Fourth, we fully develop the provisions of SS's deal in the context of these facts. SS's deal reveals that the prosecution is actively promoting perjury through its agreement with SS. Of course, SS is theoretically obligated to tell the truth about QK's robbery and stabbing. However, SS's grand jury and direct testimony insist that only he and PP were present and involved. This is demonstrably false, because QK did not pick the description of Scarface out of thin air. From the beginning, QK described the lookout as an older, tall, light-skinned African American teenage male, with a long scar on the right side of his face—Scarface. Notwithstanding the truth-telling requirement of his deal, the prosecution is sponsoring SS's perjured testimony that only he and PP were involved.

This analysis shows that there is no force to the purported truth-telling provision of the deal with SS. Functionally, all that SS is required to do is implicate PP—the young man the prosecution had already indicted—at the time SS admitted to Officer Krupke that he was the stabber. Furthermore, the prosecution is permitting a known participant in the robbery-stabbing—Scarface—to go free from apprehension and prosecution altogether. With the deal as a lever, any competent prosecutor could easily compel SS to identify, and disclose the whereabouts of, his undoubted accomplice, Scarface.

But the state is willing to forgo this truth in order to keep SS happy on the witness stand. Or, maybe, the prosecution does not want to hear what Scarface would tell them about who actually stabbed QK and who was not involved at all.

4

Tips to Prepare and Organize the Case

The actual work of Case Analysis is hard and time-consuming. Fortunately, it does not require enormous financial resources to perform—just relentless personal effort and, with luck, the help of an equally motivated investigator, trial assistant, or co-counsel.

Following are some tips on how to do this work. Obviously, whole books have been written on the subject of how to prepare a case. Here, are the highlights.

Step One: Create and Update Three Documents

1. Outcome Lever T-charts. See chapter 2, Step Two.

2. Cast lists of people and relationships in the case. Especially when our practice involves a large number of cases, just keeping the relevant participants and witnesses straight can be a real task. A cast list begins as a simple list of the names of each person involved—whether likely witnesses or not—and each one's role in the case, like *complainant (C/W),*

C/W's girlfriend, 1st officer on scene, and so on. Next, we can group the cast-list entries by relationships among the players. These could be by personal or professional relationships; by common motives, biases, and interests; by who discovered or developed them in the case; or by any number of other groupings we deem relevant. We will probably end up with several cast lists in any case. Look for and find similarities and differences among the people involved in the case to promote Case Analysis.

3. A CHRONOLOGY OF EVENTS. This includes not only a chronology of the crime or incident, but also of the subsequent investigation, interviews, reports, and litigation. Chronologies of more specific subparts may also be useful. For example, if we chart SS's criminal history and interviews sequentially and chart QK's statements, this may reveal motives and biases. Often this exercise answers the critical question: *Why* did the witness change his or her account?

   For example, witnesses may change statements over time, claiming to "know" or "remember" important facts later, which they denied or failed to report previously. Chronologies can reveal the occurrence of intervening public media reports, conversations with other civilians, or police-prosecutor interviews with the witness. These intervening events provide the basis for demonstrating influence on the witness's recall, whether intended or not.

   Similarly, arresting a witness is a common intervening factor, which results in the witness's revising his story. The same effect may happen if the witness, or her family member or friend, is the victim of a wholly unrelated crime while the case is going on. The variety and number of such influencing events is vast and requires that we conduct an intensive background and ongoing investigation of each significant witness.

Step Two: Get to Know the Physical Potential and Limits of Events

1. Get to the scene ASAP. We want to see the scene as close in time to the charged event as possible, and in comparable circumstances. If this means going there at 2:30 a.m., so be it. Being at the scene always helps us see what witnesses saw, what they assumed, what they just can't know, and what we can imagine could fit and occur there. Neither photographs nor videos can re-create a scene view—they always distort absolute and relational distances. In some cases, jury views of the scene are critical to their ability to understand the defense reality of innocence. In those cases, move for a jury view. Most judges have never done one, and they often enjoy trying it. The key is for the defense to handle all the logistics by hiring a bus to transport the jurors. It's cheap. We can easily access public area scenes, just by going there, fast. We can usually access private property scenes with polite discussion with the owner, resulting in consent. If the owner is reluctant, we can usually overcome this with appeals to fairness and by pointing out that the facts are just the facts. If necessary, a discovery request to get the DA to obtain the owner's consent may succeed.

   If QK, for example, refuses to let us inspect, measure, and photograph his store, then we can move for a court order to inspect the premises. There is no legitimate basis for refusing this access, particularly given our willingness to do the inspection after or before store hours. The legal basis for this motion may be in the Criminal Rules, Discovery Rules, or embraced in the accused's state and federal constitutional rights to compulsory process and to due process.[1]

1. *See, e.g., Fathke v. State,* 951 P.2d 1226 (Alaska App. 1998) (Crim. R. 17(c) empowers court to order third party to submit fingerprint samples for defense comparison prior to trial).

2. GET THE OPPONENT'S EVIDENCE. This could include photos, diagrams, maps, charts, audio and video recordings, documents, physical evidence, and illustrative exhibits. We will know the state's physical and demonstrative evidence better than they will. We will identify all the inaccuracies. More important, we will be ready to show how those inaccuracies provide a biased and misleading picture of what they purport to depict.

   For example, a street diagram, like the one in chapter 1, but which is not to scale, could make the distance QK ran look similar to the distance PP allegedly moved up E Street in the same time period. However, the real distance on Fourth Avenue is two and a half times greater than the distance on E Street.

3. MAKE YOUR OWN PHOTOS, MAPS, DIAGRAMS, AND EXHIBITS. Police and prosecutors photograph and illustrate the story of guilt they are telling. We often want to show different or additional things. Their depictions have the unique advantage of being close in time to discovery of the event, but ours can be of superior quality and show more context, because we have more time to prepare them.

4. RESEARCH SCIENTIFIC OR EXPERT OPINION EVIDENCE. We must research and consult experts on the limits and potentials of the scientific or expert opinion evidence. This is a book-worthy subject in its own right. For now, it is enough to say that the quality and usefulness of any expert testimony is directly proportional to the amount of work we put into preparing the referral, the detail and thoroughness of that referral, and the continuing dialogue we conduct with the expert. That dialogue precedes the referral, continues from his receipt of it, is intense between the time of his review and the filing of his report, and continues until he walks off the stand at the end of his trial testimony.

5. RESEARCH PSYCHOLOGICAL OR BEHAVIORAL EVIDENCE. We must research and consult experts on the limits and

potentials of the psychological or behavioral evidence. Often a hugely neglected area, this kind of evidence can provide a field day for creative lawyers. It is remarkable that police officers and prosecutors developed significant parts of this type of opinion testimony.

For example, self-defense cases can fail because the decedent's entry wound is in the side or back, leading to the state's claim that the deceased could not have been an aggressor. Instead, they suggest, the deceased was fleeing from the accused. Yet, in many cases, police officers have shot innocent civilians in the back and claimed self-defense but are not even prosecuted. Supporting this exercise of prosecutorial discretion is empirical research showing that in the second it takes to form the intent and pull the trigger, a previously aggressive assailant can turn partially or fully away from the weapon, resulting in a shot in his back.

6. Repeat these preparation steps throughout the case. We'll always find something new. We just have to keep looking.

Step Three: Analyze All Witness Information Statements and Testimony

We must obtain and develop a working knowledge of all information, prior statements, and prior testimony for every person who may testify for either side in the case.

This process—including identification of the steps required to make the most useful witness trial files—is discussed in detail in chapter 6 of *Dynamic Cross-Examination*[2] and is not repeated here.

2. *See Dynamic Cross-Examination, supra* chapter 1, note 1, at chapter 6.

5

Maxims for Attorneys for the Underdog

1. Every jury trial is a referendum on the human spirit.
2. Hope, innocence, and life overcome fear, vengeance, and cynicism.
3. Every case is the biggest, most important one we ever had . . . just ask our client.
4. Every human being is entitled to have at least one person in his or her corner—for most of our clients, we are that person.
5. We enjoy representing our clients, however outmanned and overwhelmed they may be.
6. Our reward is to see that they get better representation than they could buy even if they were wealthy.
7. The other side can always outspend us, but we can always outwork and outthink them.
8. There can be no fairness without courage, and there can never be justice without fairness.

9. Every case can be won—are we brave enough to really believe it? Are we disciplined enough to really go for it?
   - If we don't believe, if we blink, the jury won't believe either.
   - It takes a lot more courage to win than it does to lose.
   - We can't ask more of the jury than we do of ourselves. Neither should the court.
   - The greatest limits on advocacy are always self-imposed.
10. What we create in the courtroom, in front of the jury, has the most impact by far.
    - Pay attention all the time! Search for opportunities!
    - They are always there to be found—lots of them.
11. To a large extent, we make our own room in the courtroom.
12. Every second in the presence of the jury is an opportunity for advocacy. Use each and every one.
13. The mental demand is to develop a functional understanding of how facts, human behavior, courtroom dynamics, and the legal system fit together.
    - Organization is the most neglected form of advocacy.
14. Long, demanding representations and trials are wars of attrition. Do we have the focus and endurance, and will we pay the physical and emotional prices, necessary to win?
15. In litigation, anything can be rationalized. Don't ever do it.
    - If it makes our lives easier, it's probably the wrong choice.
16. "Hungry is he who fishes for minnows, while whales swim by." —W. Gary Kohlman

17. Collectively, a properly enabled jury is smarter than any lawyer or judge. But we construct the plausible, persuasive, factual reality, enabling them to acquit.

18. The only relevant question is "What do I need to do to win?"

    - Not—"What is less risky?"
    - Not—"What decision will be least subject to criticism?"

    Screw looking good. We've got to win the case for our client.

19. Turn honest-mistake cases into something else, anything else. Let the jurors do what they do best—dissect credibility.

20. Never lie to, deceive, mislead, misrepresent to, or be inaccurate with the judge. Refuse to respond, but do not deceive.

    But—for that, fight the judge without giving or asking any quarter.

    - Note that "get personal with" is not included in the list of prohibitions.
    - We'll use any honest thing we've got to make a judge be fair.

21. The bad part of a case won't go away just because we ignore it.

    The worse a fact, legal issue, or outcome lever is, the sooner we need to understand it, and the sooner we need to figure out how to deal with it.

22. Experience is way, way overrated. Hard work and preparation are way, way underrated.

    - Investigation, Case Analysis, preparation, and creative thinking provide the foundation for effective advocacy.

23. Persuasion is still comprised of logos, pathos, and ethos. Today, however, ethos not only includes the advocate's personal credibility, but, more important, appeals to the cultural premises of fairness, duty, and equality.

24. We trial lawyers must be fluent in three languages simultaneously:
    - The language of fact = controlled by the rules of evidence.
    - The language of persuasion = advocacy.
    - The language of the rules of decision = jury instructions.
25. We'll stay on the high road whenever we can, but no judge, no prosecutor, no cop, no witness will ever take advantage of us or our clients.
26. We'll attack or disrespect a witness only after he shows that he deserves it or asks for it by his own behavior in front of the jury or when he must be disbelieved.
    - Even then, we're firm and relentless, not out of control.
    - We always consider whether staying above the witness's level may hurt his credibility even more than duking it out.
    - Show no joy in destroying a witness in front of the jury. It's snake-killing; it's a dirty job that just needs to be done.
27. We always prepare, monitor, and correct our client's appearance and behavior in court. We prepare our client for the bad things he is likely to see and hear in trial.
28. An issue can be so two-sided that the party raising it also loses it.
29. In trial, less may be more, and more may be a bore, or worse.
30. Appropriate humor is a winner; inappropriate humor is a disaster.

31. We learn to take a punch, but we never show we're hurt.
32. Remember always—this is hard work, full of joy and hope. Find it every day, and celebrate it. Know when to declare victory.

6

Conclusion

The effective Case Analysis method in this book is the beginning and the end of effective representation, whether or not the case ultimately results in trial or some sort of plea deal or settlement. Invariably, we represent the underdog, and the underdog's opponent, who has all the resource and power advantages, fears only one thing—the embarrassment of losing at trial. Only if we prepare the strongest case for trial will we create the leverage to produce a truly desirable plea deal or settlement for our client.

The Case Analysis method provides three fundamental benefits to the trial lawyers who use it.

First, it identifies the few points for each side that, in and of themselves, can determine the outcome of the trial. Recognition of these outcome levers focuses our attention on the in-court and out-of-court phenomena that will move the jury's verdict. The same process identifies all potential trapdoors—the circumstances capable of creating a verdict against us, even though we persuade the jury to accept our basic claims.

Second, using our recognition of the outcome levers and trapdoors, we develop a plausible, persuasive factual reality that is consistent with our client's innocence.

Third, we consciously scrutinize every part of the trial process and determine how we can use each part to minimize the effect of the opponent's points, maximize the impact of our own, avoid the trapdoors in the case, and develop the content of the reality of innocence upon which our defense is based. From investigation to discovery litigation, from witness and client interviews to voir dire preparation, from pretrial motions to exclude, or admit, certain evidence to legal memos filed for the same reason during trial—every step of the process is directed and coordinated by the same, coherent Case Analysis.

Every stage of the trial process also follows our analysis—which judge to preempt, jury selection, opening statement, cross-examination, moving for judgments of acquittal or directed verdict, direct examination, preparation of jury instructions, closing arguments—we use all these to implement our Case Analysis strategy. In the book *Dynamic Cross-Examination,* I repeatedly point out, and explain how, the content of dynamic crosses comes directly from the prior, and continuing, work of our Case Analysis. Similarly, the following appendices contain case-specific detail on how to use this method of Case Analysis in practice, at every stage of the pretrial and trial process.

Case Analysis is the compass that guides us most effectively through preparing for and trying cases. It is also the source of the facts and inferences we need to develop and present to the jury in order to have the best chance of winning for our clients. Trust it. It works.

Appendices

The following appendices are taken or derived from actual cases I defended during my thirty-year career in Washington, DC, Wisconsin, and Alaska. They are intended to show how Case Analysis affects the entire defense function. Often it is the simultaneous—and always interconnected—investigative, preparatory, motion litigation, and trial processes upon which we rely to eliminate or minimize the prosecution's outcome levers while maximizing the impact of our own. We rely on those same processes to enable us to effectively present the plausible, persuasive reality of innocence to the jury. We hope to see their acceptance in a verdict of "not guilty."

Caveat: The following pleadings do not purport to reflect the current state of the law. The purpose of including them is to show how I used them as an integral part of implementing what I learned by Case Analysis when I practiced from 1978 to 2008.

Appendix A

Some Voir Dire Questions for Race Cases

Following are some voir dire questions that are useful when the client is of a minority race and is accused of killing or harming a majority-race complainant. Obviously this is not the entire voir dire on the subject, and most of the questions lead to additional discussion, based upon the answers we receive. We can use questions like this to minimize or eliminate the state's race outcome lever (P-1) in the *Piper* case.[1]

The Race Card

Q: You know, I hear people using this statement, often talking about defense lawyers, "Well, he played the race card." I don't really know what that means, but I do know if jurors think that is what we are doing, the case is lost. Does anyone here know what is meant when people say, "He played the race card"?

Q: Do you think it is possible for a prosecutor to "play the race card" in his presentation of a case? How?

Q: Please understand that we are not playing any race card in this trial. Neither Mr. P nor I are asking for—or want—any

1. The actual case underlying appendix A is the same one used as an example of an effective in-court demonstration with the complaining witness in *Dynamic Cross-Examination, supra* chapter 1, note 1, at appendix A.

special or lenient treatment because he is poor and black. Everyone clear on that?

Q: At the same time, do we all agree that you jurors in this courtroom must treat Mr. P as fairly and equally as if he looked like any of us? Why?

Limited Relevance of Race

If your case has aspects in which race is relevant—such as to show investigative bias or witness motivation to lie—discuss the permissible, but *limited,* purposes here. Also identify the impermissible uses, have jurors explain why they are impermissible, and secure convincing promises from the jurors that they will not make impermissible use of race.

Actual Racial Bias

Q: Even today, some people honestly cannot be fair jurors in cases where the accused is black and the complainant is white.

Sometimes this occurs because of the attitudes people were exposed to as children, sometimes because of their own personal experiences, sometimes for other reasons.

Often, in this age of political correctness, people are reluctant or embarrassed to discuss these things in front of others. If any of you thinks that you might not be able to be completely fair to Mr. P in this case, please raise your hand now, and we will talk to you more in private. *[Show of hands and private, individual voir dire.]*

Stereotypes

Q: Who knows what "stereotypes" are?

["Stereotypes" constitute well-learned sets of associations or expectations connecting particular behaviors or traits with members of a particular social group. See appendix B.]

Q: I'm mostly Scottish and Irish in my background. What kind of stereotypes do you think I've heard applied to me?

[Scottish: miserly. Irish: drinker and partier]

Q: How many of you have been stereotyped—at home, at work, in the community—by others because of your name, appearance, ethnic background, religion, or other factor?

[Work with each juror and elicit the stereotypes and effect.]

Q: How often are those stereotypes false or unfairly slanted?

Q: How so?

Q: Do you think that people forming stereotypical opinions are always aware that they are doing so?

[Often, we may rely on stereotypes without even being aware that we are doing so. See appendix B.]

Q: How often do you think stereotypes come into play in our daily lives?

Racial Stereotypes

Q: Now, we've talked about blondes, redheads, and Irishmen, let's look into stereotyping on the basis of race.

Q: You know we get these messages from TV, movies, books, and the news every day. Even if you fight against it, it is hard not to be influenced by racial stereotypes, and most of the time we don't even realize it.

Q: Three weeks ago, I was stopped at a red light at Fourteenth and U Streets, here in Anytown. Next thing I know a beautiful new Lexus pulls up in the lane to my right. I look over, and I see a young African American man in a hooded sweatshirt driving. The first thought that flashes in my mind is *drug dealer.*

Not *doctor's son*—or *guy who works at a dealership*—but *drug dealer*. As I thought about it, I felt sick, just sick.

I didn't think I was prejudiced before this. I tried to raise my boys to treat everyone equally, with no regard to race. So this little snapshot of my mind was so disappointing to me. But it also showed me the power of stereotyping and that we may not even be aware of its impact.

[My close friend and co-counsel Cynthia Strout, an excellent trial attorney in Alaska, did this brilliant self-disclosing part of the voir dire. It had the effect of enabling every white juror to talk candidly about racial stereotyping and led to a voir dire that successfully removed the prosecution's race outcome lever altogether.]

Q: What stereotypes have you heard about young, urban African American males?

Q: Please, forget about political correctness; let's just honestly list the behavior and traits that constitute the media stereotype of young, urban African American males.

[List all behaviors and traits on a board or pad.]

Q: Remember Susan Smith, and the many other cases—before and since—where white criminals falsely blamed black men—sometimes fictitious and sometimes real—for crimes they themselves had done?

Q: Why do people believe them?

Q: Do you think stereotypes can affect assumptions people make about parties, witnesses, or the merits in court cases?

Q: Happens every day in the media and our reactions to those opinions, doesn't it?

Q: Looking at this list, how in the world is Mr. P going to get a fair trial in this courtroom?

[This list-all-the-stereotypes technique, culminating in the challenge "How can my client get a fair trial?" was developed by Jeff Robinson, an outstanding African American attorney who practices in Seattle, Washington.]

Racial Stereotypes Must Have No Effect

Q: As a juror, will you take any racial stereotype into account in deciding the case?

[Jurors must not make assumptions about the parties and witnesses based on their membership in a particular racial group. Jurors must not assume that a particular interpretation of a person's behavior is more or less likely because the individual belongs to any particular racial group. See appendix B.]

Q: Why not?

[Reliance on stereotypes in deciding real cases is prohibited both because every accused is entitled to equal protection of law, and because racial stereotypes are historically, and notoriously, inaccurate when applied to any particular member of a race. See appendix B.

And, it is horribly unfair—remember the Golden Rule.]

How to Stop Racial Stereotypes from Affecting the Case

Q: Obviously, we cannot completely unlearn the media and cultural messages that have caused us to form racial stereotypes just by snapping our fingers.

At the same time, as jurors, you must not be influenced, however slightly, by these images. You must prevent even subconscious influence of your views in this case by racial stereotypes.

So how can you guarantee that you will be wholly unaffected by the effects of conscious or subconscious racial stereotypes?

[1. Honest awareness of the risk.

2. Conscious, constant identification and rejection of stereotypical thoughts or feelings that arise during trial and deliberations.

3. Race-switching exercises—imagine the racial reverse of the present case, and see if you feel differently about it.]

Appendix B

Special Jury Instruction: Race Switching

The following is a special jury instruction that has been given in a number of race-related cases around the country. This instruction is derived from a model instruction proposed by then associate professor C. Lee, in her article *Race and Self-Defense: Toward a Normative Conception of Reasonableness.*[1]

This instruction helps minimize the state's P-1 outcome lever—overt and covert racial bias—in the *Piper* case.

The clean copy, read to and sent back with juries, follows the proposed instruction, which is annotated with appropriate authority.

The underlying actual case is the same one referenced in appendix A of this book and in appendix A of *Dynamic Cross-Examination.*[2]

1. 81 Minn.L.Rev. 367, 482 (1996).
2. *See Dynamic Cross-Examination, supra* chapter 1, note 1, at appendix A.

Copy with Supporting Authority for the Judge

INSTRUCTION NO. ___

[ANTI-RACE-STEREOTYPE INSTRUCTION]

It is natural for human beings to make assumptions about the parties and witnesses in any case based on stereotypes.[3] "Stereotypes" constitute well-learned sets of associations or expectations connecting particular behaviors or traits with members of a particular social group. Often, we may rely on stereotypes without even being aware that we are doing so.[4] As a juror, you must not make assumptions about the parties and witnesses based on their membership in a particular racial group. You must not assume that a particular interpretation of a person's behavior is more or less likely because the individual belongs to any particular racial group.[5]

---

3. Social science research establishes that reliance on stereotypes is a common means by which people comprehend and interpret the world, particularly ambiguous interactions between people. Hofstadter, Metamagical Themas: Questioning the Essence of Mind and Pattern, 137 (1985); Krieger, *The Content of Our Categories: A Cognitive Bias Approach to Discrimination and Equal Employment Opportunity,* 47 Stan.L.Rev. 1161, 1187–89 (1995); Hamilton, *A Cognitive-Attributional Analysis of Stereotyping,* 12 *Advances in Experimental Soc. Psychol.* 52 (L. Berkowitz ed., 1979).

4. Reliance on racial stereotypes often operates at a subconscious level. C. R. Lawrence III, *The Id, The Ego, and Equal Protection: Reckoning with Unconscious Racism,* 39 Stan.L.Rev. 317, 322 (1987).

5. The black-as-violent-criminal stereotype is ingrained in, and pervades, American society. B. L. Duncan, *Differential Social Perception and Attribution of Intergroup Violence: Testing the Lower Limit of Stereotyping of Blacks,* 4 J. *Personality and Soc. Psychol.* 590 (1976) (75 percent of 104 white undergrads described black person shoving white person as "violent," 6 percent as "playing around"; only 17 percent described white person shoving black person as "violent"; 42 percent described white person as "playing around"); Sager &

Reliance on stereotypes in deciding real cases is prohibited, because every accused is entitled to equal protection of law. Also, racial stereotypes are historically, and notoriously, inaccurate when applied to any particular member of a race.[6]

To ensure that you have not made any unfair assessments based on racial stereotypes, you should apply a race-switching exercise to test whether stereotypes have affected your evaluation of the case. Race switching involves imagining the same events, the same circumstances, the same people, but switching the races of the parties and witnesses. For example, if the accused is African American and the accuser is white, you should imagine a white accused and an African American accuser.

Schofield, *Racial and Behavioral Cues in Black and White Children's Perceptions of Ambiguously Aggressive Acts,* 39 *J. Personality and Soc. Psychol.* 590 (1980) (both black and white children tend to rate relatively innocuous behavior by blacks as more threatening than similar behavior by whites); C. Lee, *Race and Self-Defense: Toward a Normative Conception of Reasonableness,* 81 Minn. L. Rev. 367, 406–10, 464 n.389 (1996) (impact of racial stereotypes in specific self-defense cases and studies of effect of stereotypes on jury function in sexual violence cases). The American media and entertainment industries perpetuate, and widely disseminate, the black-as-violent-criminal stereotype. C. Lee, *supra,* 81 Minn. L. Rev., 403 n.107.

6. White people's fear of being victimized by violent African American criminals is a case in point. In 1994, African Americans arrested for violent crimes constituted less than 1 percent of the total African American population, and less than 2 percent of male members of that group. FBI, U.S. Dept. of Justice, U.S. Uniform Crime Reports for the U.S. (1993 & 1994); Bureau of Census, U.S. Dept. of Commerce, Statistical Abstract of the U.S., 21 (1995). Overall, only 3 percent of all violent crimes involve African American defendants and white victims. Kennedy, *Comment: The State, Criminal Law, and Racial Discrimination,* 107 Harv. L. Rev. 1255 (1994).

If your evaluation of the case is different after engaging in race switching, this suggests a subconscious reliance on stereotypes. You must then reevaluate the case from a neutral, unbiased perspective.

Clean Copy for the Jury

INSTRUCTION NO. ___

It is natural for human beings to make assumptions about the parties and witnesses in any case based on stereotypes. "Stereotypes" constitute well-learned sets of associations or expectations connecting particular behaviors or traits with members of a particular social group. Often, we may rely on stereotypes without even being aware that we are doing so. As a juror, you must not make assumptions about the parties and witnesses based on their membership in a particular racial group. You must not assume that a particular interpretation of a person's behavior is more or less likely because the individual belongs to any particular racial group.

Reliance on stereotypes in deciding real cases is prohibited, because every accused is entitled to equal protection of law. Also, racial stereotypes are historically, and notoriously, inaccurate when applied to any particular member of a race.

To ensure that you have not made any unfair assessments based on racial stereotypes, you should apply a race-switching exercise to test whether stereotypes have affected your evaluation of the case. Race switching involves imagining the same events, the same circumstances, the same people, but switching the races of the parties and witnesses. For example, if the accused is African American and the accuser is white, you should imagine a white accused and an African American accuser.

If your evaluation of the case is different after engaging in race switching, this suggests a subconscious reliance on stereotypes. You must then reevaluate the case from a neutral, unbiased perspective.

Appendix C

Notice of Expert in Race Case

Dr. Psychol was prepared to testify about the psychological dynamics in this case, where more than a dozen white witnesses saw an "attack" with a deadly weapon by the sole African American teen on an older white classmate. See appendix A. However, the voir dire on race and stereotyping went so well that the good doctor was never called.

The complainant's version was destroyed on cross-examination.[1] The judge gave the race-switching instruction, contained in appendix B.

The jury acquitted of Assault-1 (a Class-A felony) and all the lesser included offenses in less than three hours, including lunch. The next day, a white, middle-aged woman juror from the front row called and left this message for us. "Thank you for representing [Albert Accused]. You have restored my faith in the justice system."

1. *See Dynamic Cross-Examination, supra* chapter 1, note 1, at appendix A.

IN THE SUPERIOR COURT FOR THE STATE OF ALASKA

____ JUDICIAL DISTRICT AT ____

STATE OF ALASKA,)

PLAINTIFF)

V.)

ALBERT ACCUSED,)

DEFENDANT.)

CASE NO. 0XX-S00-0000 CR

NOTICE OF EXPERT: PAULA PSYCHOL, PH.D.

CERTIFICATE

> I certify that this document and its attachments do not contain (1) the name of a victim of a sexual offense listed in AS 12.61.140 or (2) a residence or business address or telephone number of a victim of or witness to any offense unless it is an address used to identify the place of the crime or it is an address or telephone number in a transcript of a court proceeding and disclosure of the information was ordered by the court.

Albert Accused, by his counsel, and pursuant to Alaska Rule of Criminal Procedure 16, hereby provides notice that the defense may present the testimony of Dr. Paula Psychol, a qualified research psychologist, in its case at trial.

In making this notice, the defense states as follows:

1. Paula P. Psychol holds a PhD in experimental psychology from Super University (1971), and a BA in experimental

psychology from Fabulous University (1967). Her employments, awards, research grants, professional memberships, and publications are listed in the accompanying c.v. Dr. Psychol has qualified as an expert and testified in court in her field of expertise on numerous occasions, including in cases in the state of Alaska.

2. Her opinion in this case, and the bases for it, consist of applications of psychological principles concerning human perception, principles whose reliability is well accepted and long established in the field of psychology. These principles are relied upon daily in conducting research, training, and education in the field of psychology.
3. Her testimony in this case will consist of an explanation of the relationship between some of these principles—external (events in the world) and internal (mental model) input—in human perception of events.
4. In her experience, the extent of the influence of internal mental models on perception is beyond the ken of most of the populace at large, particularly when racial stereotypes are involved. In general, people tend to believe that if someone is in a position to perceive an external event, s/he will perceive it accurately—in the sense of external accuracy. In fact, however, the internal mental model—including subconscious racial stereotyping—may play a significant, even predominant, role in the subject's perception. Absent

expert testimony, the large majority of laypeople won't be able to understand how a large number of witnesses may interpret an ambiguous situation—such as a push or shove of an African American student by a white student—in a way that minimizes aggression, due to subconscious reliance on racial stereotypes.

5. Dr. Psychol will explain that, from a psychological point of view, such inaccuracy in perception, comprehension, and/or memory often results from subconscious reliance on stereotypes. Social science research establishes that reliance on stereotypes is a common means by which people comprehend and interpret the world, particularly ambiguous interactions between people. "Stereotypes" constitute well-learned sets of associations or expectations connecting particular behaviors or traits with members of a particular social group. Often, people rely on racial stereotypes without even being aware that they are doing so. Racial stereotypes are historically, and notoriously, inaccurate when applied to any particular member of a race.
6. The black-as-violent-criminal stereotype is deeply ingrained in American society. Psychological research shows that this stereotype often has a direct effect on how adult and child witnesses to disputes interpret what they see, to the extent that identical behavior engaged in by whites is seen as playful or nonviolent; but when engaged in by

African American subjects, the same conduct is described as violent and threatening.

7. A common application of some of these principles occurs when psychologists are called to explain the potential vagaries of eyewitness identification testimony. Dr. Psychol has qualified and testified as an expert in such cases in state and/or federal courts in Alaska, Arizona, California, Colorado, Indiana, New York, Montana, Oregon, and Washington, approximately fifty times.
8. This case simply presents another application of the same principles in the related context of perception during unexpected/ambiguous events. Dr. Psychol has qualified and testified as an expert in such cases in the courts referenced above on approximately twenty to thirty occasions.

Dated at______, Alaska, this ____ day of ________, 0000. Etc.

Appendix D

Motion for Protective Order

Accused's Uncharged Bad Acts/Crimes/Character

Following is a Motion for Protective Order/Motion *In Limine* to exclude evidence of the accused's prior bad acts, other crimes, and bad character (Evidence Rules 403 & 404(b), *inter alia*). Following the Motion is the Reply Brief, which responded to the prosecution's Partial Opposition, prior to the hearing.

When fully briefed, supported by an evidentiary hearing, if necessary, and particularly where the "legitimate" relevance is diminished or revealed to be nothing more than criminal propensity, these motions often succeed, even in the most serious, high-profile cases.

IN THE SUPERIOR COURT FOR THE STATE OF ALASKA

_____ JUDICIAL DISTRICT AT _____

STATE OF ALASKA,)

PLAINTIFF,)

V.)

CHARLIE CHARGED,)

DEFENDANT.)

CASE NO. 0XX-S00-0001 CR.

P-2

MOTION FOR PROTECTIVE ORDER: OTHER CRIMES, WRONGS, ACTS OR BAD CHARACTER AND SUPPORTING POINTS AND AUTHORITIES

CERTIFICATE

I certify that this document and its attachments do not contain (1) the name of a victim of a sexual offense listed in AS 12.61.140 or (2) a residence or business address or telephone number of a victim of or witness to any offense unless it is an address used to identify the place of the crime or it is an address or telephone number in a transcript of a court proceeding and disclosure of the information was ordered by the court.

Charlie Charged, by his counsel, respectfully moves this Court, pursuant to Alaska Rules of Evidence 401–405, 608–609, and to his state and federal rights to due process of law, art. I,

Section 7, Alaska Constitution, Amendment XIV, United States Constitution, to enter a protective order precluding the state from introducing against him evidence of, reference about, or argument on any crimes, wrongs, or acts impugning his character, which were allegedly committed by him, other than those alleged in the indictment, and/or any reference to, argument about or evidence of alleged bad character on his part.

CONTENTS

Statement of Relevant Facts

In this case, the accused is charged with First-Degree Murder, Attempted Murder, and Assault-1 for firing at four or five potential intruders as they allegedly fled from his home. Trained by the U.S. army, he killed one and wounded two others.

Summary of Original Statement of Facts

In lieu of including the lengthy statement of facts, the information most relevant to the Motion is summarized below.

In the course of searching Charlie Charged's residence after his arrest, the police found a defunct two-plant marijuana grow "operation," and some other drugs and drug paraphernalia. (There had been a fairly raucous wake the night before at his home, with eighty people in attendance. This is where the bad blood that led to the shooting began.) Also seized were various T-shirts, books, magazines, a homemade sex video, and other "drug"-related objects. These are the items referred to as "drug/drug culture" evidence in the Motion.

Police also found a small arsenal of handguns, shotguns, rifles, defunct grenades, alleged bomb parts, ammunition, cartridge reloading equipment, and full-sized *Star Wars* figures holding their futuristic weapons in a "menacing" fashion. This is what is referred to in the Motion as "unrelated 'weaponry.'"

The numerous references to paragraph and subparagraph numbers in the Motion reflect that the Statement of Relevant Facts section was lengthy, detailed, and designed to be easily accessed in the discussion without having constantly to repeat all of the details.

Finally, the police elicited the unelaborated admission from Charlie Charged that he had been "in about three fights in my life."

The defenses are self-defense and defense of home. The purpose of the Motion is to eliminate, by suppression of the evidence, the state's outcome lever that Charlie is a violent, criminal, and bad person.

I. The Rule 404 Evidence Is Inadmissible

It is a fundamental ideal of American justice that we judge people accused of crime based on what they did or didn't do, not on who they are.

> Our reluctance to sanction the use of evidence of other crimes stems from the underlying premise of our criminal justice system, that the defendant must be tried for what he did, not for who he is.

U.S. v. Bradley, 5 F.3d 1317, 1320 (9th Cir. 1993) (citation omitted). This principle finds expression in Alaska Evidence Rules 404(a) and (b).

This fundamental principle is threatened every time other crimes/bad character evidence is introduced in a criminal trial.

> [T]he danger inherent in informing a jury that a defendant has committed a prior criminal act is self-evident: it is all too likely that a determinative inference of guilt will be drawn from the fact of the prior act, thus diluting the requirement that present guilt be proved beyond a reasonable doubt.

Oksoktaruk v. State, 611 P.2d 521, 524 (Alaska 1980)

A. Evidence of the Accused's Character Is Absolutely Prohibited

With respect to direct character evidence, ARE 404(a) provides—

> Evidence of a person's character or a trait of character is not admissible for the purpose of proving that the person acted in conformity therewith on a particular occasion . . .

The accused, and the accused alone, can put his character in issue, by introducing character evidence. ARE 404(a)(1). As against the state, however, the ban on initiating evidence of an accused's character is absolute.

Thus, suggestions that Charlie is "the kind of person" who likes guns and military-type weaponry, is excited by firearms, or is interested in the subject of explosives are absolutely inadmissible in this case, unless an evidentiary connection can be made between the specific items offered and the alleged offense. *Haakanson v. State,* 760 P.2d 1030, 1035–37 (Alaska App. 1988); *Page v. State,* 657 P.2d 850, 851–53 (Alaska App. 1983); *Kvasnikoff v. State,* 674 P.2d 302 (Alaska App. 1983).[1]

B. Other Crimes/Wrongs/Acts Inadmissible to Prove Propensity

ARE 404(b) provides as follows:

> Evidence of other crimes, wrongs, or acts is not admissible if the sole purpose for offering the evidence is to prove the character of a person in order to show that the person acted in conformity therewith. It is, however, admissible for other purposes, including, but not limited to, proof of motive, opportunity, intent, preparation, plan, knowledge, identity, or absence of mistake or accident.

1. In the exceptional instances where an accused's character for certain traits may be legally relevant, prosecution proof is limited to opinion/reputation testimony; evidence of specific prior acts is precluded. *See* ARE 405(a); *Allen v. State,* 945 P.2d 1233 (Alaska App. 1998).

Thus, proof of prior conduct to prove criminal propensity is never permissible. Alaska Rules of Evidence 404(a) & (b); *Clark v. State,* 953 P.2d 159, 162–63 (Alaska App. 1998); *Haakanson v. State,* 760 P.2d 1030, 1035–37 (Alaska App. 1988); *Stevens v. State,* 748 P.2d 771, 774–76 (Alaska App. 1988). The Alaska Supreme Court has so held, making the categorical determination that unfair prejudice far outweighs the probative value of propensity evidence: "No case by case balancing is permitted; a prior crime may not be admitted to show propensity." *Oksoktaruk,* 611 P.2d, 524. *Accord Adkinson v. State,* 611 P.2d 528 (Alaska 1980).

Here, criminal propensity is the only conceivable use for the evidence identified in paragraphs 10.a. 209–10, 362–69, 376, 378–79, 384 & 401; 10.b. & 11, *Statement of Relevant Facts* [herinafter *Facts*], *supra.* Accordingly, all such evidence must be excluded at trial.[2]

C. The Scope of Material Subject to ARE 404(b) Is Broad

It is pretty obvious that "other crimes" refers to criminal activity other than that charged in the case and that "wrongs" includes conduct that could give rise to civil causes of action. But what about the "acts" referred to in ARE/FRE 404(b)?

Analysis of evidence under Rule 404 is required whether or not the evidence pertains to criminal behavior. The occasional prosecutorial claim that noncriminal acts may be admitted without satisfying the requirements of Rules 403 & 404(b) fails "as

2. ARE 404(b); *Oksoktaruk v. State, supra; Adkinson v. State, supra; Clark v. State, supra; Haakanson v. State, supra; Stevens v. State, supra.*

a matter of statutory construction and common-law analysis." Imwinkelried, *Uncharged Misconduct Evidence,* sec. 2: 15, ch. 2, p. 79 (1996). The language of the Rule 404(b) is expansive, not limited. *Id.,* sec. 2: 03, ch. 2, p. 4. This choice of language manifests a congressional intent "to apply 404(b) to any noncriminal conduct that effectively impugns the defendant's character." *Id.,* sec. 2: 15, ch.2, p. 79. Federal courts have reached the same conclusion.[3]

Any narrower view is inconsistent with the policy underlying the common-law doctrine from which Rule 404(b) arose. Whenever the nature of the evidence may prejudice the accused in the jury's eyes, thus creating the risk of conviction on an improper basis, that policy is implicated. *Imwinkelried, supra,* sec. 2: 15, ch. 2, p. 80. *Accord U.S. v. Terebecki,* 692 F.2d 1345 (11th Cir. 1982). For example, evidence that an accused frequents adult bookstores, or belongs to a radical religious group or political party, or lawfully consumes large quantities of alcohol—while constituting neither criminal nor civil law violations—certainly implicates the policies of, and is subject to, FRE 403 & 404(b) analysis. Evidence of unrelated, noncriminal sexual activities and preferences—like the sex video seized here—is invariably excluded from evidence. Alaska appellate courts have consistently required exclusion of bad sexual-character/acts evidence offered

3. *See, e.g., U.S. v. Erickson,* 75 F.3d 470, 478 (9th Cir. 1996), cert. denied, 116 S.Ct. 1853; *U.S. v. Miller,* 573 F.2d 388 (7th Cir. 1978).

by the state against the accused in sex prosecutions.[4] *See Smithart v. State,* 946 P.2d 1264, 1269–73 (Alaska App. 1997), rev'd on other grounds, 988 P.2d 584 (Alaska 1999) (accused's persistent offering rides to other young girls was ARE 404(b) evidence).

Here, all of the evidence/conduct described in paragraphs 10.a., 10.b. & 11, *Facts, supra,* is subject to ARE 403 & 404 analysis.

D. The Legal Relevance Requirement

Before evidence can be admitted, it has to be relevant. Evidence that is not relevant is not admissible. ARE 402. Relevant evidence is "that evidence which has any tendency to make the existence of any fact that is of consequence to the determination of the action more probable or less probable than it would be without the evidence." ARE 401. Rule 401 carries forward the traditional requirements that evidence must have legal relevance and

4. *Wood v. State,* 736 P.2d 363, 365–66 & n.1 (Alaska App. 1987) (evidence rape complainant posed nude in *Penthouse* and performed in X-rated movies not legally relevant to accused's consent defense); *Page v. State,* 657 P.2d 850, 851–53 (Alaska App. 1983) (sexually explicit homosexual publications in possession of defendant inadmissible against him in same-sex rape case); *Kvasnikoff v. State,* 674 P.2d 302 (Alaska App. 1983) (evidence that male rape complainant had engaged in, and had a reputation for engaging in, homosexual acts with others, excluded, notwithstanding accused's reliance on consent defense); *Heath v. State,* 849 P.2d 786, 788 (Alaska App. 1993) (evidence of the fifteen-year-old complainant's virginity and lack of prior sexual experience inadmissible); *Haakanson v. State,* 760 P.2d 1030, 1035–37 (Alaska App. 1988) (sex abuser/pedophile profile evidence inadmissible against accused; ARE 404(a)); *Stevens v. State,* 748 P.2d 771, 774–76 (Alaska App. 1988) (error, held harmless, to admit accused's statements about his sexual fantasies, including re young boys leading him to masturbate, in case charging sexual abuse of a ten-year-old boy).

materiality before being admitted over objection. *Gunnerud v. State,* 611 P.2d 69, 72 (Alaska 1980).

Evidence of the accused's other alleged criminal or character-impugning acts, substance use, or general bad character is neither legally relevant nor material to any issues raised by the indictment in this case. *See, e.g., Clark v. State,* 953 P.2d 159, 162–63 (Alaska App. 1998); *Haakanson v. State,* 760 P.2d 1030, 1035–37 (Alaska App. 1988); *Stevens v. State,* 748 P.2d 771, 774–76 (Alaska App. 1988).

Although ARE 404(b) no longer limits the permissible uses of other-act evidence to the purposes listed in the rule, the burden remains on the proponent of such evidence to prove its legal relevance and materiality. Federal courts—which have long applied an "inclusionary" other-crimes rule—do not presume such evidence to be admissible. As stated by the Ninth Circuit:

> The Government, however, must carry the burden of showing how the proffered evidence is relevant to one or more issues in the case; specifically, it must articulate precisely the evidential hypothesis by which a fact of consequence may be inferred from the other acts evidence.

U.S. v. Hisnandez-Miranda, 601 F.2d 1104, 1108 (9th Cir. 1979). *See 2 J. Weinstein & M. Berger, Weinstein's Evidence,* P. 404(08), at 404–49 (1981).[5]

5. *U.S. v. Mayans,* 17 F.3d 1174, 1181 (9th Cir. 1994); *U.S. v. Mehrmanesh,* 689 F.2d 822, 830 (9th Cir. 1982).

The Ninth Circuit has "emphasized consistently that evidence of extrinsic acts may not be introduced unless the government establishes its relevance to an actual issue in the case." *State of Arizona v. Elmer,* 21 F.3d 331, 336 (9th Cir. 1994), quoting *U.S. v. Hodges,* 770 F.2d 1475, 1479 (9th Cir. 1985). And the use of evidence pursuant to Rule 404(b) "must be narrowly circumscribed and limited." *U.S. v. Garcia-Orozco,* 997 F.2d 1302, 1304 (9th Cir. 1993). "Relevance" cannot be manufactured by prosecutorial invocation of marginal theories. *See, e.g., Pavlik v. State,* 869 P.2d 496, 498 (Alaska App. 1994) (prior bad act not admissible to explain why troopers were on site; defense not challenging bias of officers).

1. Clear and convincing evidence is required.

Until recently, the overwhelming majority of states required that, prior to admission of an accused's other crimes/bad acts, the prior misconduct be established to the trial judge's satisfaction, by clear and convincing evidence. *State v. Terrazanas,* 944 P.2d 1194, 1196 (Ariz. 1997); *Imwinkelried, supra,* sec. 2.09, at 36 & n.9. The American Bar Association's Criminal Justice Section urges nationwide adoption of the clear and convincing standard, and the A.B.A. House of Delegates has endorsed the Section's position. *Id.,* 39 & nn. 48–49.

A minority of states require only proof by a preponderance. *Id.,* sec. 2.09, at 36 & n.20. And the U.S. Supreme Court held in *Huddleston v. U.S.,* 485 U.S. 681 (1988), that other-crimes evidence was subject only to FRE 104(b)'s relaxed requirement of admission. Therefore, federal trial judges are no longer empowered to exclude such evidence on insufficiency grounds in most cases. *Huddleston,* 485 U.S., 686–89. Subsequently, the Court approved admission of evidence of a prior crime for which the accused has been previously acquitted. *Dowling v. U.S.,* 493 U.S.342, 348–54 (1990).

Huddleston has not been well received by most state courts, and numerous states continue to depart from it, either by legislative action or judicial construction of state evidence provisions. Despite *Huddleston,* many states continue to require that trial judges find other crimes to be proven by clear and convincing evidence before they may be admitted in evidence.[6] Other states adhere to standards functionally similar to, or more demanding than, the "clear and convincing" evidence standard.[7]

6. *See, e.g., State v. Terrazas,* 944 P.2d 1194, 1196–98 (Ariz. 1997); *Johnson v. U.S.,* 683 A.2d 1087, 1092–93 (D.C.App. 1996), *cert.den.,* 520 U.S. 1148 (1997); *Phillips v. State,* 591 So.2d 987, 989–90 (Fla.Dist.Ct.App.1st Dist. 1991); *State v. Jackson,* 625 So.2d 146, 149 (La. 1993); *Ayers v. State,* 645 A.2d 22, 37 (Md. 1994); *State v. Spaeth,* 552 N.W.2d 187, 193, 195 (Minn. 1996); *State v. Wilson,* 556 N.W.2d 643, 652 (Neb. App. 1996); *Daniel v. State,* 923 P.2d 728, 734 (Wyo. 1996); *State v. McCary,* 922 S.W.2d 511, 514 (Tenn. 1996); *Winiarz v. State,* 820 P.2d 1317, 1321 (Nev. 1991); *State v. Smith,* 387 S.E.2d 245, 247 (S.C. 1989).

7. *See, e.g., State v. Cohen,* 634 A.2d 380, 386 (Del.Super. 1992) ("plain, clear and conclusive"); *State v. Howell,* 557 N.W.2d 908, 911 (Iowa App. 1996) ("clear proof"); *State v. Michaud,* 610 A.2d 354, 356 (N.H. 1992) ("clear proof; firmly establishing"); *Harrell v. State,* 884 S.W.2d 154, 157 (Tex.Crim. App. 1994) (en banc) ("clear proof" is the same as "proof beyond a reasonable doubt" standard); *State v. Wilson,* 423 S.E.2d 473, 476 (N.C.App. 1992) ("substantial evidence").

Even state courts that settle for the lower preponderance standard reject *Huddleston*'s elimination of the trial judge's threshold role in determining if that standard has been met.[8]

In Alaska, these basic questions have not been dispositively answered. Alaska appellate courts have upheld admission of prior acts for which the accused was never charged or convicted, but there has been no clear statement of what the standard of proof is for such acts, nor of the court's authority to exclude other crimes that are insufficiently proven. *State v. Bingaman,* 991 P.2d 227, 229 & n.6 (Alaska App. 1999). Alaska cases decided subsequent to *Huddleston* have neither adopted nor rejected its standard/process of proof holding.[9]

Although not yet decided, it seems apparent from the close scrutiny to which Alaska appellate courts have always subjected Rule 404 evidence, that the Alaska Supreme Court will require, at least, that trial judges find "clear and convincing evidence" before admitting such evidence. Moreover, given the pretrial notice and litigation requirements of ARE 404(a)(2)(i)–(iii) & (b)(2), 608(c) & 609(c), of nearly every superior court pretrial order, and of *Moor v. State,* 709 P.2d 498, 505–6 (Alaska App. 1985), it seems certain that the Alaska Supreme Court will reject

8. *See, e.g., State v. McGinnis,* 455 S.E.2d 516, 526–28 (W.Va. 1994); *People v. Garner,* 806 P.2d 366 (Colo. 1991).

9. *Huddleston* was cited in *Clark v. State,* 953 P.2d 159, 162 (Alaska App. 1998), and in *Velez v. State,* 762 P.2d 1297, 1310 (Alaska App. 1988). *Dowling* has only been cited in *Allen v. State,* 945 P.2d 1233, 1239 (Alaska App. 1997).

Huddleston's diminution of the role of trial judges in determining, prior to admission, the sufficiency of such evidence.

Here, there is considerable doubt as to whether the state can connect the multitude of items it removed from Charlie's residence to him, by any standard of proof. For instance, the semiautomatic rifle, with scope and tripod, belongs to, and was possessed by, Charlie's tenant, Richie Renter. And the minimal, fragmentary evidence of purported drug residue in "pipes" and canisters throughout the residence seems much more probative of there having been eighty guests over the night before than of Charlie's possession of the items.

2. Drug evidence **not** *relevant to homicide counts*

Much of the evidence proffered against Charlie cannot satisfy the demands of legal relevance. The evidence of alleged marijuana growing and possession/use of other drugs has no legal relevance in this murder case. Alaska appellate courts have so held, for decades. *See Gould v. State,* 579 P.2d 535, 538–40 (Alaska 1978) (evidence of accused's heroin addiction not relevant in armed robbery case; reversed); *Eubanks v. State,* 516 P.2d 726, 728–29 (Alaska 1973) (evidence accused bought heroin with proceeds not relevant to charged grand larceny; reversed); *Toomer v. State,* 890 P.2d 598, 600 (Alaska App. 1995) (no "affirmative link" or "particularized connection" between cocaine use and charged offense; Theft-2 reversed). As the Court said in *Gould,* evidence of drug use is legally relevant in an assault-type crime only "when there exists some affirmative link between the crime and the use or addiction." *Gould,* 579 P.2d, 538. "'To admit such testimony without showing some affirmative link between the [other crime] and narcotics would show only that the accused is a criminal generally.'" *Id.* (citation omitted).

Federal courts have reached the same conclusion.[10]

Thus, the drug-use and drug-culture evidence identified in paragraph 10.a., *Facts, supra,* is not legally relevant to any of the homicide counts and must be excluded.

3. Unrelated weaponry/fights not *relevant to any counts*

It is equally well established that weapons and prior assaults, which are not specifically connected to the charged offenses, are irrelevant and inadmissible. *Brown v. State,* 601 P.2d 221, 226–27 (Alaska 1979); *Lerchenstein v. State,* 697 P.2d 312, 315 (Alaska App. 1985), aff'd, 726 P.2d 546 (Alaska 1986); *Stern v. State,* 827 P.2d 442, 445 (Alaska App. 1992) (accused's unrelated gunfight the night before charged shooting and recent release from prison inadmissible).[11]

10. *See, e.g., U.S. v. Blackstone,* 56 F.3d 1143 (9th Cir. 1995) (drug paraphernalia inadmissible in weapons case; reversed); *U.S. v. Labansat,* 94 F.3d 527, 530–31 (9th Cir. 1996), cert. denied, 519 U.S. 1140 (1997) (drug use/possession inadmissible in bank robbery prosecution); *U.S. v. Madden,* 38 F.3d 747 (4th Cir. 1994) (same; reversed).

11. *Accord U.S. v. Himmelwright,* 42 F.2d 777, 782–85 (3d Cir. 1994) (accused's possession of handguns not relevant to some counts, and, at best, arguably marginally relevant to others in extortionate threat/intent to injure by wire case; reversed); *U.S. v. Murray,* 103 F.3d 310, 317–18 (3d Cir. 1997), cert. denied, 525 U.S. 91 (1998) (prior shooting-murder irrelevant in CCE-murder prosecution; no evidentiary link between criminal enterprise's purposes and other act).

Here, most of the other, unrelated weaponry items were properly secured behind a twice-padlocked door, and many were locked in a gun safe behind that door. How such items could be legitimately linked to Charlie's response to the decedent's and complainants' unannounced burglary at his residence defies even the most active imagination. Thus, the items described in paragraph 10.b., *Facts* lack legal relevance because they played no role in the shooting and must be excluded.

Obviously, Charlie's "about three" prior, unelaborated "fights" while growing up have no actual relevance to his response to repeated invasions and aggressions by the intruding gang. *Lerchenstein v. State,* 697 P.2d 312, 315 (Alaska App. 1985), aff'd, 726 P.2d 546 (Alaska 1986); *Stern v. State,* 827 P.2d 442, 445 (Alaska App. 1992).

The unrelated weaponry/fights evidence is probative of nothing more than inadmissible and improper general criminal propensity/bad character inferences. Accordingly, exclusion of this evidence from trial is mandatory. *See* Sections I.A. & B., *supra.*

E. The Risk of "Unfair Prejudice" and the ARE 403 Balance

1. The meaning and reality of the "risk of unfair prejudice"

Even if evidence is relevant, it must be more probative than unfairly prejudicial. ARE 403. Evidence is "unfairly prejudicial" "if it has an undue tendency to suggest a decision on an improper basis such as emotion or character rather than evidence presented on the crime charged." *U.S. v. Joetzki,* 952 F.2d 1090, 1094 (9th Cir. 1991).

a. The meaning of "unfair prejudice"

In *Old Chief v. U.S.*, 519 U.S. 172, 117 S.Ct. 644 (1997), the Court held that it was an abuse of discretion, in a felon-in-possession-of-firearm case, for the trial judge to admit the name and nature of the accused's prior conviction instead of accepting his admission that he had previously been convicted of a felony. The Court explained, "The term 'unfair prejudice,' as to a criminal defendant, speaks to the capacity of some concededly relevant evidence to lure the factfinder into declaring guilt on a ground different from proof specific to the offense charged." *Old Chief*, 117 S.Ct., 650. The Court further identified some of the ways an accused may suffer unfair prejudice:

> Such improper grounds [for conviction] certainly include . . . generalizing a defendant's earlier bad act into bad character and taking that as raising the odds that he did the later bad act now charged (or, worse, as calling for preventive conviction even if he should happen to be innocent momentarily).

Old Chief, 117 S.Ct., 650.

Even if a general inference of bad character is not drawn, generic similarity between the other act and the nature of the conduct on trial may lead to a more specific inference of criminal propensity to commit certain kinds of crimes. *Old Chief*, 117 S.Ct., 652. The Advisory Committee Notes to FRE 403 also identify an "emotional" basis for a verdict as an improper ground. Federal Criminal Code & Rules, at 244 (West 1998 Edition).

Courts have expressed additional concerns about the potential for prejudice inherent in evidence of unrelated bad acts/bad character. Some observe that jurors will give such evidence too much weight, regardless of the other evidence. *See Michelson v. U.S.*, 335 U.S. 469, 475–76 (1948). Other courts recognize that such evidence may functionally eliminate the presumption of innocence, *U.S. v. Myers*, 550 F.2d 1036, 1044 (5th Cir. 1977), and/or lower the bar of what constitutes proof beyond a reasonable doubt. *Oksoktaruk v. State*, 611 P.2d 521, 524 (Alaska 1980).[12]

b. The empirical reality of unfair prejudice

For decades, empirical research has validated these concerns. Studies from the London School of Economics indicate that, all other factors remaining constant, admission of an accused's uncharged misconduct significantly increases the likelihood that a jury will find him guilty. *Imwinkelried, supra*, Sec. 1: 03, at 6 n.7 (West Group 1999). Even earlier, the Chicago Jury Project demonstrated that, as a practical matter, the presumption of innocence operates only for defendants who have no criminal record. Kalven & Zeisel, *The American Jury*, 160–61, 178–79 (1966).[13] Proof of other crimes causes jurors to place accused persons within a "criminal" stereotype and predisposes jurors to convict

12. *Accord* Natali & Stigall, *"Are You Going to Arraign His Whole Life?": How Sexual Propensity Evidence Violates the Due Process Clause*, 28 Loyola U. Chi. L. J. 1, 11–12 (1996).

13. By "no criminal record" the authors mean no criminal record that is admitted in evidence, and thus known to the jury.

"them." When such evidence is presented, the jury will probably use a "different . . . calculus of probabilities" in deciding whether to convict. Kalven & Zeisel, *supra,* 179.

A study sponsored by the National Science Foundation Law & Social Science program confirms the conclusions reached by the London School and the University of Chicago.[14]

Similarly, it is well established that mock juror ratings of a defendant's guilt are higher when crimes are joined than when the offenses are tried separately. Greene and Loftus, *When Crimes Are Joined at Trial,* 9 Law & Human Behavior 193 (1985).[15]

In his classic work, *Convicting the Innocent,* at xv–xvi (1932), Prof. Borchard conducted a detailed inspection of sixty-five cases in which factually innocent citizens were wrongfully convicted. In many of the cases he studied, the admission of other-crimes evidence was "fatal" to the innocent defendants' chances for acquittal. *Id.* Other-crimes evidence and "criminal" stereotyping have also been instrumental in erroneous police decisions to target, prosecutorial decisions to charge, and/or jury decisions to

14. *See* Teitelbaum, Sutton-Barbera & Johnson, *Evaluating the Prejudicial Effect of Evidence: Can Judges Identify the Impact of Improper Evidence on Juries?* 1983 Wis.L.Rev. 1147. The impact of such evidence appears in civil litigation as well. Where civil juries learn of a plaintiff's criminal record, he will likely receive a verdict 16 percent below the national average for such cases; on the other hand, if the civil defendant has a record, the plaintiff's verdict will increase by 9 percent. *Herbert & Berrett, Attorney's Master Guide to Courtroom Psychology,* 320–21.

15. *Accord* Tannford, Penrod & Collins, *Decision Making in Joined Criminal Trials: The Influence of Charge Similarity, Evidence Similarity, and Limiting Instructions,* 9 Law & Human Behavior 319 (1985).

convict hundreds of accused people who were later determined to be factually innocent. *Radelet, Bedau & Putnam, In Spite of Innocence,* at 26, 30, 39, 87, 96–97, 177, 232, 237–38, 247–48, 250, 286, 298, 304, 308, 315, 333, 337–39, 342 (1992).

Finally, a study conducted at Boston College graphically demonstrates the disproportionate impact even "limited" other-crimes evidence has on jurors. One hundred sixty randomly selected "jurors" were asked to render a verdict in a hypothetical murder case. The only variable was the nature of the testifying defendant's prior conviction—either for perjury or for attempted murder. Although all jurors were instructed to use the prior conviction solely in assessing the defendant's credibility, the results were as follows: 60 percent voted to convict where the prior conviction was for perjury, but 75 percent convicted when the prior was for attempted murder. Thus, jurors improperly used the prior attempted-murder conviction for bad man/bad character/propensity inferences, even when specifically instructed not to do so. Wissler & Saks, *On the Inefficacy of Limiting Instructions—When Jurors Use Prior Conviction Evidence to Decide Guilt,* 9 Law & Human Behavior 37, 43 (1985).

Accordingly, "the weight of available [empirical] studies supports the traditional doctrine" that jurors are likely to misuse and overemphasize other-crimes evidence introduced against the accused. *Imwinkelried, supra,* Sec. 1.03, 13.[16]

16. *Accord* Beaver & Marques, 58 Temp.L.Q. 585, 602 (1985) ("As part of the University of Chicago Jury Project, Dale Broeder interviewed jurors after

2. Application of law to facts

Where the evidence necessarily informs the jury of character-impugning conduct allegedly committed by the accused—other than that charged in the indictment—the prejudice is presumed to outweigh the legitimate probative value. ARE 404(b); *Lerchenstein v. State,* 697 P.2d 312 (Alaska App. 1985), *aff'd,* 726 P.2d 546 (Alaska 1986).[17] The risk of prejudice increases when the prior conduct is generically similar to, or includes, or is included in, the kind of conduct at issue in the trial. *Id.; Velez v. State*, 762 P.2d 1297 (Alaska App. 1988).[18]

they had deliberated and rendered verdicts in criminal trials. Reporting his findings, Broeder asserted that the 'jurors almost universally used the defendant's record to conclude that he was a bad man and hence was more likely than not guilty of the crime for which he was then standing trial.'"); Note, *Social Science Findings and the Jury's Ability to Disregard Evidence Under the Federal Rules of Evidence,* 52 Law & Contemp.Probs. 341, 347–48 (1989) (jurors' inability to understand instruction not to take a defendant's prior record as evidence of his criminal propensity "may have led to the jurors' inability to follow limiting instructions given them"); Note, *Character Evidence by Any Other Name . . . A Proposal to Limit Impeachment by Prior Conviction Under Rule 609,* 58 Geo.Wash.L.Rev. 762, 764, 789, 791 (1990) ("Studies and surveys support the view that a jury is likely to give substantial consideration to prior convictions in assessing the defendant's guilt, despite instructions to the contrary"; "numerous studies and articles . . . support . . . [the] conclusion that there is an 'overwhelming tendency for jurors . . . to misuse prior conviction evidence.'"); Note, *Enhancing Penalties by Admitting "Bad Character" Evidence During the Guilt Phase of Criminal Trials—State v. Bishop,* 1989 Utah L.Rev. 1013,1017–19 (summarizing the studies).

17. Indeed, an individual cannot be prosecuted in a single trial for an offense and for being a felon in possession of a firearm; the prejudice to him on the substantive count of informing the jury that he has a prior felony conviction requires severance or bifurcation of the charges as a matter of law. *Elerson v. State,* 732 P.2d 192 (Alaska App. 1987).

18. Invariably, the state cites the 1991 amendments to ARE 404(b) in support of its claim that the rule became one of "inclusion." But the difference between

Even in the federal system, the required balancing necessitates exclusion of unfairly prejudicial bad act/bad character evidence, notwithstanding the existence of some legitimate relevance. This is true of unrelated weaponry.[19] And it is true of unrelated drug activity.[20]

---

a rule of "exclusion" and one of "inclusion" does not have anything to do with the presumption of prejudice at the ARE 403 weighing stage. The federal rule, which the legislature sought to emulate, has long been known as a rule of "inclusion," simply because the categories of nonpropensity purposes listed therein were construed as exemplary, not exhaustive. The statement of legislative purpose confirms that the new Alaska rule of inclusion accepts evidence for nonpropensity purposes other than those listed in the rule. Ch. 79, § 1(c), SLA 1991; *Peratrovich v. State,* 903 P.2d 1071, 1074 (Alaska App. 1995) ("the legislature's declared purpose in amending the rule was to expand the scope of admissibility").

Nothing about the amendment of ARE 404(b) affects the balancing requirement of ARE 403. Lerchenstein's presumption—that unfair prejudice outweighs the legitimate probative value of Rule 404 evidence offered against an accused—continues to be good law. This aspect of the Lerchenstein holding remains unaffected by the amendment's recognition of a wider scope of permissible nonpropensity purposes. *See, e.g., Smithart v. State,* 946 P.2d 1264, 1271 (Alaska App. 1997) (citing Lerchenstein with approval on issue of balancing under ARE 403); *Johnson v. State,* 889 P.2d 1076, 1081 (Alaska App. 1995) (citing Lerchenstein with approval on issue of balancing under ARE 403); *Pavlik v. State,* 869 P.2d 496, 499 & n.1 (Alaska App. 1994) (reserving question of whether 404(b) amendments affect Lerchenstein holdings).

19. *U.S. v. Himmelwright,* 42 F.2d 777, 785–87 (3d Cir. 1994) (any marginal relevance of accused's purchase and possession of handguns outweighed by unfair prejudice in extortionate threat/intent to injure by wire case; reversed); *U.S. v. Murray,* 103 F.3d 310, 317–18 (3d Cir. 1997), *cert. denied,* 525 U.S. 91 (1998) (any assumed relevance of prior shooting murder in CCE-murder prosecution outweighed by risk of unfair prejudice; reversed).

20. *U.S. v. Vizcarra-Martinez,* 66 F.3d 1006 (9th Cir. 1995) (personal drug use too prejudicial in prosecution for manufacture of same drug; reversed); *U.S. v. Blackstone,* 56 F.3d 1143 (9th Cir. 1995) (evidence of drug paraphernalia inadmissible in weapons prosecution; reversed); *U.S. v. Aguilar-Aranceta,* 58 F.3d 796 (1st Cir. 1995) (misdemeanor drug conviction relevant to knowledge, but too prejudicial in possession with intent to distribute case; reversed).

None of the unrelated weaponry items described in para. 10.b., *Facts,* even comes close to satisfying the Rule 403 balancing test, and their enormous potential for generating unfair prejudice against the accused necessitates their exclusion as to both the homicide and drug counts.

As for the drug evidence, the risk of unfair prejudice substantially outweighs any theoretical probative value, at least with respect to the items specified in paragraph 10a. 209–10, 362–69, 376, 378–79, 384, and 401.

F. Constitutional Considerations and ARE 403 & 404(b)

Where, as here, extreme unfair prejudice would result from the admission of other crimes, wrongs, acts and/or character evidence, exclusion is mandated by the Alaska Constitution. *See, e.g., Oksoktaruk v. State,* 611 P.2d 521, 524 (Alaska 1980) (improper admission will "dilut[e] the requirement that present guilt be proved beyond a reasonable doubt"); *Adkinson v. State,* 611 P.2d 528, 531 (Alaska 1980) (improper admission denies right to defend against particular crime charged).

Similarly, federal due process is denied when admission of bad acts evidence deprives the accused of a fundamentally fair trial. *See, e.g., McKinney v. Rees,* 993 F.2d 1378 (9th Cir. 1993); *Walker v. State,* 703 F.2d 959 (6th Cir. 1983); *Bryson v. Alabama,* 634 F.2d 862 (5th Cir. 1981); *Foster v. Watkins,* 423 F. Supp. 53 (W.D.N.C. 1976).

Conclusion

For the reasons stated herein and for such other reasons as may appear to the Court, the defense asks that Motion P-2 be granted, and that the accompanying Order be entered.

An evidentiary hearing on Motion P-2 is requested.

Dated at ____, Alaska, this ___ day of ____, 0000.

Respectfully submitted,

CHARLIE CHARGED, Defendant,

LORI LAWYER, Attorney At Law.

__________________ Anystate Bar No. 0000000

VERIFICATION BY COUNSEL

STATE OF ALASKA

THIRD JUDICIAL DISTRICT

LORI LAWYER, having been duly sworn, hereby deposes and states as follows:

1. My name is Lori Lawyer, and I am counsel of record for defendant in the above-captioned case.
2. I personally prepared the foregoing P-2, Motion for Protective Order: Other Crimes, Wrongs, Acts or Bad Character.
3. I believe the facts contained in the Statement of Relevant Facts section of the P-2 Motion, *supra,* to be true and correct, based upon my review of the discovery materials, the grand jury transcript, an independent defense investigation, and reasonable inferences therefrom.

IN THE SUPERIOR COURT FOR THE STATE OF ALASKA

___ JUDICIAL DISTRICT AT ___

STATE OF ALASKA,)

PLAINTIFF,)

V.)

CHARLIE CHARGED,)

DEFENDANT.)

CASE NO. 0XX-S00-0001 CR.

REPLY TO STATE'S RESPONSE TO P-2,

MOTION FOR PROTECTIVE ORDER:

OTHER CRIMES, WRONGS, ACTS OR BAD CHARACTER

CERTIFICATE

I certify that this document and its attachments do not contain (1) the name of a victim of a sexual offense listed in AS 12.61.140 or (2) a residence or business address or telephone number of a victim of or witness to any offense unless it is an address used to identify the place of the crime or it is an address or telephone number in a transcript of a court proceeding and disclosure of the information was ordered by the court.

Charlie Charged, by his counsel, respectfully submits the following facts, analysis, and authority in Reply to the state's Response to, and in further support of, his P-2 Motion.

What Is No Longer in Dispute

The state concedes the inadmissibility of the items described in Att. A to the P-2 Motion—drugs & drug culture evidence—in the homicide prosecution. Resp., 1–2 & state's proposed Order. This includes a purportedly homemade sexual video. *Id.* The state further acknowledges that evidence of any prior, unrelated fights involving the accused is inadmissible. Accordingly, subsections (1) & (3) of the defense's proposed Order should be granted as conceded.

Unrelated Weaponry Evidence Is Inadmissible

A. ARE 404(b) Is Applicable

The state asserts there is no prejudice in introducing Charlie's extensive weapons collection, purportedly illegal "bomb" components, shooting target illustrated like a policeman, etc. Resp., 2. A simple review of the way this evidence was presented in the grand jury proceedings—GJ, 165–76—shows the prejudice. By this "evidence," the state seeks to paint Charlie as a Timothy McVeigh clone, an ex-army militarist and gun nut who is likely to be a killer.

As shown in section I.C. of the original P-2 Motion, the scope of material subject to ARE 404(b) is broad. Rule 404(b) analysis "appl[ies . . .] to any noncriminal conduct that effectively impugns the defendant's character." Imwinkelried, *Uncharged Misconduct Evidence,* sec. 2: 15, ch.2, p. 79 (1996). For example, in *Smithart v. State,* 946 P.2d 1264, 1269–73 (Alaska App. 1997), rev'd on other grounds, 988 P.2d 584 (Alaska 1999) the court applied Rule 404(b) analysis to the state's evidence that the accused had offered rides to, and/or driven back and forth in front of, other young girls who resembled the decedent. Plainly, the inflammatory, unrelated weapons evidence here is subject to such scrutiny.

B. No Legitimate Relevance

Alternatively, the state asserts this evidence is "*res gestae* evidence and tends to show the defendant's plan and preparation." Resp., 2. How in the world can items that are secured behind a padlocked basement door, and most of which are in a locked gun safe behind that door, constitute the *res gestae* of an alleged crime in which a different weapon is fired from the upstairs living room? By what possible logic can items so secured be probative of the accused's "plan" and "preparation" to meet an assault initiated by the decedent and his gang while the accused was sleeping? The state's conclusory assertion of probity finds no support in the facts of this case.

Law, as well as logic, defeats the state's claim. Weapons that are not specifically connected to the charged offenses are irrelevant and inadmissible. *Brown v. State,* 601 P.2d 221, 226–27 (Alaska 1979); *Stern v. State,* 827 P.2d 442, 445 (Alaska App. 1992) (accused's unrelated gunfight the night before charged shooting and recent release from prison inadmissible).[21] The state responds to none of this authority and offers none of its own.

21. *Accord U.S. v. Himmelwright,* 42 F.2d 777, 782–85 (3d Cir. 1994) (accused's possession of handguns not relevant to some counts, and, at best, arguably marginally relevant to others in extortionate threat/intent to injure by wire case;

The unrelated weaponry evidence is probative of nothing more than inadmissible and improper general bad character/criminal propensity inferences. Accordingly, exclusion of this evidence from trial is mandatory. *See, e.g., Clark v. State,* 953 P.2d 159, 162–63 (Alaska App. 1998); *Haakanson v. State,* 760 P.2d 1030, 1035–37 (Alaska App. 1988); *Stevens v. State,* 748 P.2d 771, 774–76 (Alaska App. 1988).

C. Huge Risk of "Unfair Prejudice"

Where the evidence necessarily informs the jury of character-impugning conduct allegedly committed by the accused other than that charged in the indictment, the prejudice is presumed to outweigh any legitimate probative value. ARE 404(b); *Lerchenstein v. State,* 697 P.2d 312 (Alaska App. 1985), *aff'd,* 726 P.2d 546 (Alaska 1986). The risk of prejudice increases when the prior conduct is generically similar to, or includes, or is included in, the kind of conduct at issue in the trial. *Id.; Velez v. State,* 762 P.2d 1297 (Alaska App. 1988).

Even if there is a modicum of relevance to Rule 404(b) evidence, the required balancing necessitates exclusion of unfairly

---

reversed); *U.S. v. Murray,* 103 F.3d 310, 317–18 (3d Cir. 1997), cert. denied, 525 U.S. 91 (1998) (prior shooting-murder irrelevant in CCE-murder prosecution; no evidentiary link between criminal enterprise's purposes and other act).

prejudicial bad act/bad character evidence. This is true of unrelated weaponry. *See, e.g., Brown v. State,* 601 P.2d 221 (Alaska 1979).[22]

D. Constitutional Considerations

The state ignores the facts and authority showing that admission of unrelated weaponry here would generate extreme unfair prejudice and undermine Charlie's right to due process of law. *See, e.g., Oksoktaruk v. State*, 611 P.2d 521, 524 (Alaska 1980); *Adkinson v. State*, 611 P.2d 528, 531 (Alaska 1980).[23]

Conclusion

For the reasons stated herein and for such other reasons as may appear to the Court, the defense asks that Motion P-2 be granted and that the previously filed proposed Order be entered.

An evidentiary hearing on Motion P-2 is requested.

Etc.

22. *U.S. v. Himmelwright,* 42 F.2d 777, 785–87 (3d Cir. 1994) (any marginal relevance of accused's purchase and possession of handguns outweighed by unfair prejudice in extortionate threat/intent to injure by wire case; reversed); *U.S. v. Murray,* 103 F.3d 310, 317–18 (3d Cir. 1997), *cert. denied,* 525 U.S. 91 (1998) (any assumed relevance of prior shooting murder in CCE-murder prosecution outweighed by risk of unfair prejudice; reversed).

23. *McKinney v. Rees,* 993 F.2d 1378 (9th Cir. 1993); *Walker v. State,* 703 F.2d 959 (6th Cir. 1983); *Bryson v. Alabama,* 634 F.2d 862 (5th Cir. 1981); *Foster v. Watkins,* 423 F. Supp. 53 (W.D.N.C. 1976).

Appendix E

Effective Limiting Jury Instructions

Following are examples of effective jury instructions that limit jury consideration of highly prejudicial matter.

The first instruction is appropriate for the *Piper* case, if the accused testifies and is impeached with either or both of his prior adjudications (depending on the jurisdiction). Notice how this jury instruction includes all four of the elements of an effective limiting instruction, which were enumerated in chapter 2, Step Three: Maximize or Minimize Outcome Levers (page 21). The second instruction involves a case where the defendant pled guilty and was sentenced in federal court for Mail Fraud arising out of a scheme to defraud. Later, this scheme formed the basis of his state court Murder-1 prosecution. Did the instruction work? It must have done its job, as the case resulted in a complete acquittal in a very prosecution-biased venue.

As with all proposed jury instructions, the clean copy accompanies the copy with the authority for giving it, so that the Court can just pick it out and put it in the final jury packet without encountering the logistics of retyping. Of course, if modifications are made, we happily produce another, modified clean copy.

Copy with Supporting Authority for the Judge

INSTRUCTION NO. ___

[LIMITING INSTRUCTION: DEFENDANT'S PRIOR ADJUDICATIONS/CONVICTIONS]

You have heard evidence that the defendant has previously been adjudicated for two crimes, which would have been felonies if he had been an adult.

This evidence may only be considered by you to the extent, if any, it may affect his believability as a witness. You must not use this evidence for any other purpose. Specifically, you may not consider this evidence as proof of guilt of the charge(s) for which the defendant is now on trial, nor that he is a person of bad character.

The reason for this rule is that we try people for what they have allegedly done now, not for who they may have been in the past. Predictions of behavior based on past conduct are often completely wrong. Such speculation is not permitted here in this court.

Accordingly, it would be improper and unfair for you to consider Mr. Piper's prior record as any proof, however slight, of his present guilt. To do so would violate your juror's oath.

Suggested Use Note

This instruction is designed for situations in which prior convictions are admissible against an accused solely to impeach credibility. Admission of such evidence for other purposes pursuant to ARE 404(b) is addressed separately.

Upon the request by the defense, this instruction must be given. (ARE 105) Except where failure to instruct would be plain error, it should not be given over defense objection.

The instruction should be given at the time the evidence is elicited, so that the jurors do not misuse the evidence pending the final charge. The instruction should also be included in the final charge upon the request, or with the acquiescence, of the defense.

Authority

Para. 2: ARE 609, 404(a)(1) & 404(b)(1).

Paras. 3 & 4: *Old Chief v. U.S.,* 519 U.S. 172, 117 S.Ct. 644 (1997); *Oksoktaruk v. State,* 611 P.2d 521, 524 (Alaska 1980); *Adkinson v. State,* 611 P.2d 528 (Alaska 1980); *U.S. v. Bradley,* 5 F.3d 1317, 1320 (9th Cir. 1993). *Accord* analysis & authority in the P-2 Motion & Reply.

Admission of inadequately limited other-crimes evidence violates the Due Process Clauses of both the U.S. and Alaska Constitutions. *Garceau v. Woodford,* 275 F.3d 769, 775–76 (9th Cir. 2001); *McKinney v. Rees,* 993 F.2d 1378, 1384–85 (9th Cir.), cert. denied, 510 U.S. 1020 (1993); *Fields v. State,* 629 P.2d 46, 49 (Alaska 1981); *Oksoktaruk,* 611 P.2d, 524; *Adkinson,* 611 P.2d, 531.

Clean Copy for the Jury

INSTRUCTION NO. ___

You have heard evidence that the defendant has previously been adjudicated for two crimes, which would have been felonies if he had been an adult.

This evidence may only be considered by you to the extent, if any, it may affect his believability as a witness. You must not use this evidence for any other purpose. Specifically, you may not consider this evidence as proof of guilt of the charge(s) for which the defendant is now on trial, nor that he is a person of bad character.

The reason for this rule is that we try people for what they have allegedly done now, not for who they may have been in the past. Predictions of behavior based on past conduct are often completely wrong. Such speculation is not permitted here in this court.

Accordingly, it would be improper and unfair for you to consider Mr. Piper's prior record as any proof, however slight, of his present guilt. To do so would violate your juror's oath.

Copy with Supporting Authority for the Judge

INSTRUCTION NO. ___

[MAIL FRAUD SCHEME LIMITING INSTRUCTION]

Ladies and gentlemen, you have heard evidence concerning Mr. Defendant's plea of guilty in early 0000 to a single count of mail fraud in federal court in Anytown. You may only consider evidence relating to the mail fraud for the limited purpose of determining what, if any, effect it may have on the issue of motive in this case. You must not consider it for any other reason.

Specifically, you may not use the federal case as any evidence that Mr. Defendant admitted that he killed his wife, nor that the federal case determined that he did. In fact, Mr. Defendant made no such admission, and the federal court made no finding at all as to whether Mrs. Defendant's death was caused by an accident or a homicide.

In our system, we base verdicts on the sufficiency or insufficiency of evidence, not on speculation about a person's propensity or character. Opinions about guilt or innocence that are based in any part on the accused's supposed character or propensity are notoriously inaccurate and unreliable.

For these reasons, you must not use the mail-fraud evidence as tending to show that Mr. Defendant, who committed mail fraud, is likely to commit other crimes, nor that he is likely to kill anyone. You must not consider the mail fraud as tending to show that Mr. Defendant is a bad man, nor a dishonest man. You must not consider the mail fraud as tending to affect the believability or sincerity of any pretrial statements made, or conduct done, by Mr. Defendant. It would be improper and unfair for you to use the mail-fraud evidence for any of these purposes. You must not do so.

Whenever an accused person's prior conviction is admitted, there is a danger of unfair prejudice. The danger is that the presumption of innocence and/or requirement that the state prove the present charge beyond a reasonable doubt will be diluted by consideration of the prior conviction. We must not allow that danger to affect this case. We must have a truly fair trial. By your jurors' oaths, you all promised to follow my instructions, and those oaths include following this instruction. It is vital that you keep your promises to do so.

Authority

General: Pattern J. I.–Criminal, No. 1.25, Use Note; Ev.Rs.E. 105; 403; 404(a); 404(b) & 608(b).

Para. 3, sn-1: *Fields v. State,* 629 P.2d 46, 49 (Alaska 1981).

Para. 3, sn-2: Imwinkelried, *Uncharged Misconduct,* Secs. 1: 02, 6; 1: 03, 13; 2: 19, 105–7 (West Group 1999 & Pocket Part).

Para. 4, sn-1: *Oksoktaruk v. State,* 611 P.2d 521, 524 (Alaska 1980); *Carpentino v. State,* 38 P.3d 547, 550–52, state's petn. den., 42 P.3d 1137 (Alaska App. 2002).

Para. 4, sn-2: *Adkinson v. State,* 611 P.2d 528, 531 (Alaska 1980); *Bingaman v. State-II,* 76 P.3d 398, 414–15 (Alaska App. 2003); *Accord Old Chief v. U.S.,* 519 U.S. 172, 180–82 (1997).

Para. 4, sn-3: ARE 608(b). Commentary to ARE 608(b): "The second sentence [of 608(b)] bars the use of evidence of specific incidents to impeach or support the credibility of a witness" unless specifically admissible under, *e.g.*, ARE 609 or 611.

The Commentary to ARE 608(b) also notes that Fed.Rs.Evid. does not contain this prohibition. *Id.*

Para. 5, sn-1: *Oksoktaruk v. State,* 611 P.2d 521, 524 (Alaska 1980); *Bingaman v. State-II,* 76 P.3d 398, 414–15 (App. 2003).

Admission of inadequately limited other-crimes evidence violates the Due Process Clauses of both the U.S. and Alaska Constitutions. *Garceau v. Woodford,* 275 F.3d 769, 775–76 (9th Cir. 2001); *McKinney v. Rees,* 993 F.2d 1378, 1384–85 (9th Cir.), cert. denied, 510 U.S. 1020 (1993); *Fields v. State,* 629 P.2d 46, 49 (Alaska 1981); *Oksoktaruk v. State,* 611 P.2d 521, 524 (Alaska 1980); *Adkinson v. State,* 611 P.2d 528, 531 (Alaska 1980).

Clean Copy for the Jury

INSTRUCTION NO. ____

Ladies and gentlemen, you have heard evidence concerning Mr. Defendant's plea of guilty in early 0000 to a single count of mail fraud in federal court in Anytown. You may only consider evidence relating to the mail fraud for the limited purpose of determining what, if any, effect it may have on the issue of motive in this case. You must not consider it for any other reason.

Specifically, you may not use the federal case as any evidence that Mr. Defendant admitted that he killed his wife, nor that the federal case determined that he did. In fact, Mr. Defendant made no such admission, and the federal court made no finding at all as to whether Mrs. Defendant's death was caused by an accident or a homicide.

In our system, we base verdicts on the sufficiency or insufficiency of evidence, not on speculation about a person's propensity or character. Opinions about guilt or innocence that are based in any part on the accused's supposed character or propensity are notoriously inaccurate and unreliable.

For these reasons, you must not use the mail-fraud evidence as tending to show that Mr. Defendant, who committed mail fraud, is likely to commit other crimes, nor that he is likely to kill anyone. You must not consider the mail fraud as tending to show that Mr. Defendant is a bad man, nor a dishonest man. You must not consider the mail fraud as tending to affect the believability or sincerity of any pretrial statements made, or conduct done, by Mr. Defendant. It would be improper and unfair for you to use the mail-fraud evidence for any of these purposes. You must not do so.

Whenever an accused person's prior conviction is admitted, there is a danger of unfair prejudice. The danger is that the presumption of innocence and/or requirement that the state prove the present charge beyond a reasonable doubt will be diluted by consideration of the prior conviction. We must not allow that danger to affect this case. We must have a truly fair trial. By your jurors' oaths, you all promised to follow my instructions, and those oaths include following this instruction. It is vital that you keep your promises to do so.

Appendix F

Motion to Admit Witness Misconduct

Following is a Motion to Admit the prior misconduct of Sucha Snitch and Scarface on behalf of the defense in the *Piper* case. Notice how multiple bases for admission are argued. Once the evidence is admitted—say, to show witness bias—the defense is entitled to argue any reasonable inference from it—including the guilt of the witness for the crimes charged against the accused. *See* Sec. I.E, *infra.*

This pleading is a combination of pleadings used in numerous cases with a great deal of success in getting the desired other-suspect evidence, inferences, and argument admitted at trial.

Material, particularly in Section B, has been left in, although it could be excised from this motion dealing solely with Sucha Snitch. It remains, however, because there is no telling where in the vast area of bias a case's facts will lead.

This analysis and authority is useful on more than other-suspect issues. We can effectively use it as the basis of a trial memo on the scope of bias, motive, and interest cross-examination, filed a day or two before questioning begins, in order to comply with notice requirements, preempt prosecution objections at trial, and promote judicial restraint during our use of the information in cross-examination.

IN THE SUPERIOR COURT FOR THE STATE OF ALASKA

FOURTEENTH JUDICIAL DISTRICT AT ANYTOWN

STATE OF ALASKA,)

PLAINTIFF,)

V.)

PETER PIPER,)

DEFENDANT.)

CASE NO. 0XX-00-0003 CR.

OS-1

MOTION IN LIMINE:

TO ADMIT EVIDENCE, INFERENCE & ARGUMENT

THAT STATE WITNESS SUCHA SNITCH COMMITTED THE

CHARGED CRIMES.

CERTIFICATE

I certify that this document and its attachments do not contain (1) the name of a victim of a sexual offense listed in AS 12.61.140 or (2) a residence or business address or telephone number of a victim of or witness to any offense unless it is an address used to identify the place of the crime or it is an address or telephone number in a transcript of a court proceeding and disclosure of the information was ordered by the court.

Peter Piper, by his counsel, and pursuant to ARE 404(b)(1), 403, and his state and federal constitutional rights to due process, to present evidence, and to confront the witnesses called against him, respectfully asks this Court to permit introduction of the evidence specified below, which concerns the prior activities and relationships of the state's key cooperating witness, Sucha Snitch.

CONTENTS

D. Admissible to Raise Doubt Whether Sucha Snitch and Scarface Did the Stabbing and Robbery

E. Even When the *Smithart-II* Standard Is Not Met, the Defense Is Entitled to Argue Reasonable Inferences, from Otherwise Admissible Evidence, That Particular Persons May Have Committed the Crimes Charged

F. ARE 403 Favors Admission of Defense 404(b)(1) Evidence

G. The Constitutional Entitlement to Prove Innocence

Statement of Relevant Facts

[Insert here the relevant facts from the Piper *case. Whether to detail the Case Analysis, defense theory, and reality of innocence counsel has created at this point will depend on the importance of getting the motion granted and the need to educate the judge to understand why granting the motion is essential to the defense.]*

The specific information the defense seeks to admit is as follows: Sucha Snitch served six months at TYC and is on juvenile probation for another three years, having been adjudicated for armed robbery when he was twelve.

The armed robbery involved Sucha Snitch's holding up his teacher at knifepoint after school in the classroom and stealing her purse. The teacher described an African American accomplice, who stood lookout at the door of the classroom. The teacher described Sucha Snitch's lookout as a tall, light-skinned, older teen, who had a long scar running down the right side of his face. She reported that, after Sucha Snitch forced her to the wall with the knife, he grabbed her purse, and both boys then ran away. She was never shown pictures of the lookout—it appears he was never caught.

Sucha Snitch was arrested for making four sales of crack cocaine to undercover officers in his school's parking lot. As part of his deal, these schoolyard crack sales are being reduced to one count of simple cocaine possession, resulting in another concurrent probation.

I. A Witness's Prior Crimes and Misconduct Are Admissible on Multiple Bases

A. The Evidence Is Admissible to Impeach General Credibility

Under ARE 609, this Court has the authority to introduce the felony-equivalent armed-robbery adjudication to impeach the general credibility of Sucha Snitch. Given that the details of Sucha Snitch's deal with the authorities will come out in any event, this adjudication will be known to the jury. Thus, there is no legitimate interest in refusing to permit it to be considered against Sucha Snitch's testimonial credibility in general. Accordingly, the adjudication is admissible under ARE 609.

B. The Evidence Is Admissible to Prove Crime/Status Bias

The accused's right to cross-examine an opposing witness on his prior crimes and related status is fundamental and subject to very, very few limitations.

1. The constitutional entitlement

The primary purpose of the state and federal rights to confrontation is to ensure that the accused has the opportunity for meaningful cross-examination.

> . . . [A]ttack on the witness's credibility is effected by means of cross-examination directed toward revealing possible biases, prejudices, or ulterior motives of the witness. . . . [E]xposure of a witness's motivation in testifying is a proper and important function of the constitutionally protected right of cross-examination.

Davis v. Alaska, 415 U.S. 308, 316–17 (1974). The right of confrontation is of "paramount significance" and pierces the witness's claim to statutory privacy rights or privileges. *Id.*, 319 (juvenile probation status).[1]

Improper curtailment of defense cross-examination violates the Confrontation Clause. *Delaware v. Van Arsdall*, 475 U.S. 673, 680 (1986). The defendant in a criminal case is constitutionally entitled to inquire into a broad range of prior misconduct by state witnesses and their relationships with the authorities.

2. The "cooperating" witness entitlement

The defense is accorded particularly broad latitude when cross-examining informants—witnesses who have cooperation agreements

---

1. *Accord Wood v. State,* 837 P.2d 743, 747 (Alaska App. 1992); *Daniels v. State,* 767 P.2d 1163 (Alaska App. 1989) (minor witness's own criminal activity); *Sledge v. State,* 763 P.2d 1364 (Alaska App. 1988) (juvenile's ward status); *Salazar v. State,* 559 P.2d 66, 79 (Alaska 1976).

with the state or have received, or expect to receive, immunity, pay, or other benefits from the state. It is by now axiomatic that defense counsel are entitled to broad latitude in cross-examining accomplices, informers, and other "cooperating" witnesses, precisely because of the inherent danger that such witnesses will warp the truth.[2]

3. Witness bad acts/crimes are admissible on bias

A witness's prior bad acts must be admitted when probative of the witness's bias against the accused and/or motive to influence the testimony of another. *Beltz v. State,* 895 P.2d 513, 518–19 (Alaska

2. Half a century ago, the U.S. Supreme Court considered whether the inherent risk of unreliability in the testimony of such cooperating witnesses justified exclusion of their testimony altogether. In dicta in *On Lee v. U.S.,* 343 U.S. 747 (1952), Justice Jackson rejected the exclusionary remedy, endorsing instead "broad latitude" on cross-examination and appropriate jury instructions. *Id.,* 343 U.S., 757.

A decade later, in *Hoffa v. United States,* 385 U.S. 293 (1966), the Supreme Court formally accepted the use of informer-type witnesses in federal criminal trials. Although recognizing that such witnesses almost invariably have selfish motives to give false testimony, the Court held that the "established safeguards" of "rigorous cross-examination" and cautionary jury instructions were sufficient. *Id.,* 385 U.S., 311. The Court approved the "wide latitude" afforded defense counsel during his weeklong cross-examination of the key informant, which included "matters that are normally excludable," such as decades-old criminal charges that never resulted in prosecution. *Id.,* 385 U.S., 311 n.12. *See, e.g., U.S. v. Isaac,* 134 F.3d 199, 204 (3d Cir. 1998) ("broad latitude"); *U.S. v. Vargas,* 933 F.2d 701, 704 (9th Cir. 1991) ("very wide latitude," including numerous arrests); *U.S. v. Lynn,* 856 F.2d 430, 433 (1st Cir. 1988) ("especially broad latitude"); *U.S. v. Uramoto,* 638 F.2d 84, 86 (9th Cir. 1980) ("wide latitude"). This mandate for broad cross-examination of state witnesses has been embedded in Alaska case law for decades. *See Smithart v. State-II,* 988 P.2d 583, 588–89 (Alaska 1999) (other-suspects); *Evans v. State,* 550 P.2d 830, 836–37 (Alaska 1976) (informant); *Fresneda v. State,* 483 P.2d 1011, 1014 n.6 (Alaska 1971).

App. 1995) (preclusion of cross-examination of SAM complainant's mother re her prior armed assault on accused; reversed).

This principle applies equally to noncriminal "misconduct." For example, notwithstanding the high potential for prejudice, the accused is constitutionally entitled to cross-examine regarding the bisexual relationship between a state witness and the complainant in order to show the witness's bias. *McIntyre v. State,* 934 P.2d 770 (Alaska App. 1997).[3]

Similarly, where a witness's bad acts are inconsistent with the witness's trial testimony as to facts or motivations, they may be explored on cross-examination.[4]

4. Prior/current state or police involvement is admissible

Bias may also be proven by establishing the existence of a relationship between the witness/the state or the witness/the court at a relevant time. The "relevant time" for purposes of the witness's bias commences on or before the date of the offense, extends through the pretrial period during which the witness is providing information to police and prosecutors, and continues through the witness's testimony in court. Here, then, the "relevant time" for witness motive/bias/interest information commences no later

3. *See also Olden v. Kentucky,* 488 U.S. 227, 230–33 (1988) (*per curiam*) (witness's interracial cohabitation admissible); *Bibbs v. State,* 814 P.2d 738 (Alaska App. 1991) (admitting evidence of complainant's prior sexual experience).
4. *Napoka v. State,* 996 P.2d 106 (Alaska App. 2000) (minor complainant's past sexual encounters with accused admissible); *Kitchens v. State,* 898 P.2d 443 (Alaska App. 1995) (complainant's postevent demeanor, rehearsal of grand jury testimony, and "carefree" return to state admissible).

than ____, 0000, and runs through trial. Of course, the bias evidence need encompass only a portion of the relevant time in order to be admissible. *Wood v. State,* 837 P.2d 743 (Alaska App. 1992) (deferred prosecution agreement in force during time of witness's pretrial statements to authorities admissible, even though expired by time of trial testimony).

Proof that the witness is or has been held in custody during the relevant time is admissible. *Alford v. U.S.,* 282 U.S. 687, 693 (1931). Similarly, a witness's placement in protective custody or witness protection is admissible. *U.S. v. Librach,* 520 F.2d 550 (8th Cir. 1975), cert. denied, 429 U.S. 939 (1976); *U.S. v. Partin,* 493 F.2d 750, 757–60 (5th Cir. 1974), cert. denied, 434 U.S. 903 (1977). Of course, special treatment while in custody is admissible. *U.S. v. Boyd,* 55 F.3d 239, 244–46 (7th Cir. 1995) (otherwise improper telephone privileges, visits with women (including sex), and presents; new trial order affirmed); *Chavis v. North Carolina,* 637 F.2d 213, 225–26 (4th Cir. 1984). Constructive custody—like the relationship between the state and one of its wards—is also admissible, confidentiality provisions notwithstanding, where the relationship provides a juvenile witness with a bias or motive to favor the state against the accused in a criminal case. *Sledge v. State,* 763 P.2d 1364 (Alaska App. 1988).

Cross-examination demonstrating that a witness is or has been on probation or parole at a time relevant to the case must be permitted. *Davis v. Alaska,* 415 U.S. 308 (1974). This rule applies even in the absence of any demonstrable effect of the witness's status on his testimony. *Kameroff v. State,* 926 P.2d 1174, 1178–80 (Alaska App. 1996) (reversible error). Similarly, the accused is entitled to examine witnesses who are pending sentencing in unrelated criminal cases to determine their bias and interest. *U.S. v. Iverson,* 637 F.2d 799 (D.C. Cir. 1980), rehearing denied, 648 F.2d 737 (D.C. Cir. 1981).

The fact that a witness has, or had at a relevant time, an unrelated criminal case pending against him is an appropriate area for examination, whether or not any explicit promises were made by the police or prosecutors in connection with the present case. *Kyles v. Whitley,* 514 U.S. 419, 442 n.13 (1995); *Wood v. State,* 837 P.2d 743, 747 (Alaska App. 1992) (reversible error).[5]

Significantly, Alaska appellate courts have consistently held that such cross-examination must be permitted regardless of whether or not the state has provided or promised the witness a benefit in his own case for testifying against the accused. *Braund v. State,* 12 P.3d 187 (Alaska App. 2000). "[T]he test is the witness' expectation or hope of reward, not the actuality of a promise by the State."[6]

---

5. *Washington v. U.S.,* 461 A.2d 1037 (D.C.App. 1983); *Johnson v. U.S.,* 418 A.2d 136 (D.C.App. 1980); *U.S. v. Bonanno,* 430 F.2d 1060 (2d Cir. 1970), *cert. denied,* 400 U.S. 964 (1971).
6. *Accord Wood v. State,* 837 P.2d 743, 747 (Alaska App. 1992); *Mustafoski v. State,* 954 P.2d 1042, 1047 (Alaska App. 1998).

Even if no charges have been formally brought, the fact of a witness's arrest during the relevant time is admissible. *U.S. v. Croucher,* 532 F.2d 1042, 1044–46 (6th Cir. 1976) (limiting cross-examination of informer to arrests for impeachable offenses; reversed).[7]

Similarly, information that the witness has committed, or is suspected of having committed, unrelated crimes may be inquired into, in order to establish apprehension of possible prosecution and/or expectation or hope for leniency or benefit should the witness provide information/testimony against the accused in the present case. *Whitton v. State,* 479 P.2d 302, 317 (Alaska 1970). "Cross-examination to show bias because of expectation of immunity from prosecution is one of the safeguards essential to a fair trial . . ." *RLR v. State,* 487 P.2d 27, 44 (Alaska 1971).

The defense is entitled to use information that state witnesses are, or were at relevant times, the subject of investigation by law enforcement authorities concerning unrelated matters. *Kyles v. Whitley,* 514 U.S. 419, 442 n.13 (1995); *Jackson v. State,* 695 P.2d 227 (Alaska App. 1985) (accused had constitutional right to cross-examine accomplice concerning unrelated, uncharged murder in which accomplice was a suspect).[8] The Alaska Supreme Court recognizes the defense entitlement to demonstrate that a

7. *U.S. v. Garcia,* 531 F.2d 1303, 1306–7 (5th Cir.), *cert. denied,* 429 U.S. 941 (1976) (mere arrest by government may well imply bias or prejudice); *Hart v. U.S.,* 565 F.2d 360 (5th Cir. 1978).

8. *Accord Greene v. Wainwright,* 634 F.2d 272 (5th Cir. 1981); *U.S. v. Hitchmon,* 609 F.2d 1098 (5th Cir. 1979).

"state witness, who has no prosecution pending, . . . has committed criminal acts which the state knows about." *Whitton,* 479 P.2d, 317. Thus, with respect to uncharged illegal activities by state witnesses, "the mere possibility of future criminal charges is sufficient to open the area." *Evans v. State,* 550 P.2d 830, 839 (Alaska 1976).

The Court of Appeals extended this principle, and reversed a first-degree sexual abuse conviction, in *Daniels v. State,* 767 P.2d 1163 (Alaska App. 1989). Daniels knew of the complainant's uncharged sexual abuse of another minor and sought to cross-examine on the subject to show the complainant's motive to falsely accuse him. Although unknown to law enforcement authorities, the *Daniels* court held the accused was entitled to cross-examine about the prior misconduct to try to show bias.

Moreover, a witness's use/abuse of drugs may be inquired into on cross-examination to establish the witness's fear of potential prosecution or expectation of immunity in the event the witness cooperates in the present case. *Evans v. State,* 550 P.2d, 840; *Fields v. State,* 487 P.2d 831, 845–47 (Alaska 1971).

5. Witness employment by state or police is admissible

Employment relationships that involve, or are affected by, state or law enforcement authorities are also appropriate areas for cross-examination. Broad latitude is required in permitting the defense to establish the inception, circumstances of, extent of, and remuneration for *prior, unrelated informant activities* by state witnesses. *RLR v. State,* 487 P.2d, 43–44; *Evans v. State,* 550 P.2d, 835, 839. Motives to obtain or recover employment statuses with law-enforcement authorities are always appropriate areas of inquiry.[9]

6. Common prosecutorial objections are invalid

a. The preclusion-is-a-"reasonable-limit" fallacy

The prosecution typically argues that precluding all inquiry concerning a witness's prior misconduct is a "reasonable limit" on cross-examination. This contention is completely wrong—"reasonable limits" on bias cross-examination *never* include preclusion of all questions in an entire subject area.

In *Wood v. State,* 837 P.2d 743, 747 (Alaska App. 1992), the Court "carefully distinguished between the imposition of 'reasonable limits' on inquiry and the prohibition of 'all inquiry into' specific areas of possible bias." In *Wood,* the trial judge's "complete

9. *Accord Springer v. United States,* 388 A.2d 846 (D.C.App. 1978). The defense must be permitted to show that a witness is or has been "deeply involved in working for the police, which could create the material inference that [the witness] might be biased in favor of the prosecution." *Braham v. State,* 571 P.2d 631, 647 (Alaska 1977).

Hutchings v. State, 518 P.2d 767 (Alaska 1974) (defense entitled to show that undercover witness had been discharged as police officer and was seeking reinstatement at times relevant to the case). In this regard, prior criminal charges or convictions, which would not otherwise be admissible and which occurred prior to the offense charged in the present case, may be presented to the jury where relevant to show a witness's bias. When the "professed ambition" of the witness may be affected by police or prosecutor perceptions of a "serious blot" arising from prior misconduct, an inference that the witness may shape or exaggerate his testimony to gain official favor arises and may be presented by the defense. *Evans v. State,* 550 P.2d, 839–40.

preclusion of inquiry into [the witness's] conduct agreement" was an unconstitutional abuse of discretion, requiring reversal of the resultant conviction. 837 P.2d, 748–49.[10]

As an evidentiary matter, a witness's potential biases in, and motives for, testifying are "always relevant;" they are "never . . . collateral" *McIntyre v. State,* 934 P.2d 770, 773 (Alaska App. 1997).[11] And "exposure of a witness' motivation in testifying is a proper and important function of the constitutionally protected right of cross-examination." *Davis v. Alaska,* 415 U.S., 316–17.

Even when the proffered line of bias inquiry may generate "really extreme" and "enormous" prejudice to the state, it may not be categorically precluded. *McIntyre v. State,* 934 P.2d 770, 773 (Alaska App. 1997). In *McIntyre,* the Court held that the accused was entitled to cross-examine the complainant and a corroborating state witness regarding their same-sex romantic relationship. *Id.*

b. The other-available-means fallacy

Sometimes the state opines that total preclusion of a misconduct-bias inquiry can be justified because other means are available for attacking the witness's credibility, such as impeachment with prior inconsistent statements and prior convictions, and/or bias

10. The U.S. Supreme Court made the same point in *Delaware v. Van Arsdall,* 475 U.S. 673, 679 (1986). *Accord Olden v. Kentucky,* 488 U.S. 227, 230–33 (1988) (*per curiam*) (reversed).

11. *Wood v. State,* 837 P.2d, 745; *Jackson v. State,* 695 P.2d 227, 230 (Alaska App. 1985).

inferences from a favorable plea bargain. Like the preclusion-is-a-"reasonable-limit" fallacy, this second theory has long since been rejected as a matter of law.

The state's other-available-means rationale was explicitly rejected in *McKinzy v. Wainwright,* 719 F.2d 1525, 1529 (11th Cir. 1983). *McKinzy* was quoted with approval in *Wood v. State,* 837 P.2d 743, 749 n.4 (Alaska App. 1992), where the Court held that a limited inquiry into facts underlying a potential bias theory "cannot be deemed to offset the improper restriction of Wood's right to inquire [directly] into the issue of motive."

Similarly, reversal was required in *McIntyre v. State,* 934 P.2d 770, 773 (Alaska App. 1997), notwithstanding the existence of other means for discrediting the state's witnesses. Since "no other evidence [was] available to establish the same bias, a court may not wholly exclude inquiry into the [witnesses' same-sex romantic] relationship." *Id.*

c. The ARE 403 balance does not preclude cross-examination

Even when cross-examination is permitted in an area sufficient to satisfy constitutional demands, it may not be unnecessarily curtailed. As noted in Section I.B2., *supra,* the accused must be permitted broad latitude in confronting accomplice, informer, and immunized witnesses. Such cross-examination will often, necessarily, and properly, include "matters that are normally excludable." *Hoffa v. U.S.,* 385 U.S., 311 n.12.

Properly applied, ARE 403 authorizes easier admission of prior misconduct evidence when the accused is the proponent and a state informer, alleged accomplice, or other-suspect is the subject of the evidence. See Section I.F., *infra.*

7. Application to defense proffer

As the foregoing shows, Mr. Piper is constitutionally entitled to confront Sucha Snitch with the details of the bargain he struck with the state, his probation status, the crimes that will never be charged as a result, his immediate release from custody after testifying, and any other expectations he may have as a result of his "cooperation." Thus, the information contained in paragraphs 1 and 3 in the proffer in the Statement of Relevant Facts must be admitted during cross-examination of Sucha Snitch.

C. Admissible to Show Bias Protecting Accomplice

Here there is a unique, factual form of additional bias, which requires admission, not only of the fact of Sucha Snitch's adjudication for armed robbery of his teacher, but also of the specific details of that attack.

Sucha Snitch insisted under oath at his plea that only he and Mr. Piper were involved in the robbery. On the other hand, Mr. Kwiktrigger has always reported the participation of a lookout, who accompanied Sucha Snitch both times he came to the store—before and during the robbery. Mr. Kwiktrigger swore to this in the grand jury, and he described the lookout with Sucha

Snitch as "an older teen, light-skinned, and with a scar running down the right side of his face." That is exactly the same description given by Sucha Snitch's teacher of the lookout who stood at her classroom door while Sucha Snitch robbed her at knifepoint two years ago. In neither the prior robbery nor the Kwiktrigger robbery was this scar-faced participant ever identified, let alone apprehended. On the other hand, Sucha Snitch has been caught each time.

It is apparent that the criminal relationship between Sucha Snitch and "Scarface" includes the younger man's protection of the older. The jury is entitled to know this reason why Sucha Snitch is flatly contradicting Kwiktrigger and falsely insisting that no older, tall, light-skinned, right-side scar-faced robber was involved. *See McIntyre v. State,* 934 P.2d 770 (Alaska App. 1997). *See also Olden v. Kentucky,* 488 U.S. 227, 230–33 (1988) (*per curiam*); *Bibbs v. State,* 814 P.2d 738 (Alaska App. 1991).

D. Admissible to Raise Doubt Whether Sucha Snitch and Scarface Did the Stabbing and Robbery

Additionally, and independently, the details of the prior robbery are admissible as other-suspect evidence—to raise a reasonable doubt whether Sucha did the stabbing, stole the pants, and was assisted, as before, by his buddy with the scar.

Alaska courts have long grappled with the question of when to allow the accused to introduce evidence tending to show that an "other suspect" is responsible for the crime charged against the accused. Reversing Murder-1 and Sex Assault-1 convictions, the Alaska Supreme Court settled this issue in *Smithart v. State-II,* 988 P.2d 583, 586, 591 (Alaska 1999).

In *Marrone v. State,* 359 P.2d 969, 984–85 (Alaska 1961), the Supreme Court held that evidence of a third person's motive to kill, and threats against, a decedent was, in and of itself, insufficient to connect the third person to the offense. Since the foundation was insufficient, the other person's motive and threats were inadmissible. Before other-suspect evidence can be admitted to show someone else's guilt, the Court held, there must be "other evidence tending to directly connect such other person with the actual commission of the crime charged." *Id.* In *James v. State,* 671 P.2d 885, 892–94 (Alaska App. 1983), rev'd on other grounds, 698 P.2d 1161 (Alaska 1985), the Court of Appeals held that *Marrone's* "directly connect" standard is satisfied when the defense shows the other suspect "was present at the scene of the offense when it occurred or otherwise had the opportunity to commit the crime." *James,* 671 P.2d, 893. The Court specifically rejected state arguments for a more demanding standard, stating, "To require more would in effect . . . establish a requirement of independent proof [of the third party's guilt] rather than corroboration [of the defendant's contention.]" *Id.*

In a short-lived opinion apparently retreating from the *James* formulation, the Court of Appeals purported to require proof of a "substantial possibility" that the other suspect actually committed the offense charged against the accused. *Smithart v. State-I,* 946 P.2d 1264 (Alaska App. 1997). However, the Alaska Supreme Court disagreed and reversed appellant's convictions. *Smithart v. State-II,* 988 P.2d 583 (Alaska 1999).

The *Smithart-II* court found the lower court's construction of *Marrone* "too narrow" and held that other-suspect evidence "is admissible as long as it tends to create a reasonable doubt as to the defendant's guilt." *Smithart v. State-II,* 988 P.2d, 587. Thus, the Court focused the admissibility inquiry on the impact of the evidence on the case against the accused, instead of on the actual guilt of the other suspect.[12] Any implication in this Court's prior order that the defense has to proffer evidence, which will establish a reasonable doubt as a matter of law—as opposed to tending to show such doubt—must be understood as being inadvertently limiting. After all, if the defense's other-suspect evidence actually creates a reasonable doubt in the case, the Court is required to enter a judgment of acquittal.[13]

12. *See Johnson v. U.S.,* 552 A.2d 513, 517 (D.C.App. 1989), quoted with approval in *Smithart v. State-II,* 988 P.2d, 588 & n.22 (emphasis in original). *Accord Smithart v. State-II,* 988 P.2d, 590 ("orange paint evidence is relevant because it tends to create a reasonable doubt").

13. The appellate standard for reversal for erroneously excluding such other-suspect evidence requires that the exclusion be "harmless beyond a reasonable doubt"—a showing that is necessarily made by only a "reasonable possibility" that the jury could have had a reasonable doubt, based on the evidence. *Smithart v. State-II,* 988 P.2d, 589, 591.

So what evidence "tends" to create a reasonable doubt? Of course, proof of motive alone, opportunity alone, or "very attenuated evidence" alone can properly be excluded. *Smithart-II,* 988 P.2d, 588. On the other hand, any other-suspect evidence that tends to raise a reasonable doubt as to the accused's guilt must be admitted at trial. *Id.* Here, as in *Smithart-II,* the defense's proffer "combine[s] [Sucha Snitch's] opportunity, consciousness of guilt," admitted participation, a spontaneous confession to stabbing Kwiktrigger, and an eyewitness description of both Sucha and Scarface. *Compare Smithart-II,* 988 P.2d, 588.

Other-suspect proof may, of course, consist of circumstantial evidence—including the other person's prior crimes, violent acts, and/or violent character. *See Garner v. State,* 711 P.2d 1191, 1192–94 (Alaska App. 1986) (other-suspect's prior assault on a different child admissible).[14] *Cf. Keith v. State,* 612 P.2d 977,

14. *Accord U.S. v. Vallejo,* 2001 U.S.App. Lexis 7367, 7369 (9th Cir. 2001) (prior vehicle owner's drug involvement admissible to support inference that he, not accused, had secreted drugs in the car accused was driving); *Carriger v. Stewart,* 132 F.3d 463, 481 (9th Cir. 1997) (*en banc*) (other-suspect's history of violence); *U.S. v. Brooke,* 4 F.3d 1480, 1488–89 (other crimes tending to show other-suspect was acting on his own but blaming other patsies); *U.S. v. Calle,* 822 F.2d 1016, 1021 (11th Cir. 1987) (other-suspect's major drug-dealing activities admissible to support inference suspect, not defendant, was the true source of cocaine); *Com. v. Thompson,* 779 A.2d 1195, 1201–2 (Pa. Super. 2001) (vehicle driver's prior drug involvements admissible to show he, not defendant, constructively possessed cocaine); *State v. Clark,* 898 P.2d 854, 856, 858–59 (Wash. App. 1995) (threat to torch a *different* building admissible). *Accord State v. Hamons,* 805 P.2d 6, 12–13 (Kansas 1991) (circumstantial evidence admissible in case where state's evidence is circumstantial), cited with approval in *Smithart v. State-I,* 946 P.2d, 1277–78; *State v. Hawkins,* 260 N.W.2d 150 (Minn. 1977) (reversible error to exclude other-suspect's prior

982–83 (Alaska 1980) (decedent's journal, showing volatile and violent mental state/personality, admissible).[15]

In *Smithart-II,* the Supreme Court utilized *Garner* to "illustrate the reasons that the trial court's *Marrone* ruling was too narrow." 988 P.2d, 587–88 & n.20.[16] *Garner* is particularly important here, because it required admission of other-crimes evidence about an other-suspect, without much more. *Id.,* 1193–95. Defending against the charge of murdering his minor stepson, Garner sought to introduce evidence that his neighbor had, on prior occasions, physically abused her own child.[17] *Id.,* 1193–94.

---

acts of violence when drinking against persons other than decedent), quoted with approval in *Smithart v. State-II,* 988 P.2d, 588–89.

15. The specific probative force—and admissibility—of a decedent's reputation for, and/or prior acts of, violence has long been recognized in self-defense cases. *Gottschalk v. State,* 881 P.2d 1139 (Alaska App. 1994); *Amarok v. State,* 671 P.2d 882 (Alaska App. 1983). The same admissibility principle now applies to the accused's prior conduct. *Allen v. State,* 945 P.2d 1233, 1237–42 (Alaska App. 1997) (applying ARE 404(a)(2). And, in upholding admission of pure propensity evidence even against an accused under ARE 404(b)(2)-(4), the intermediate court has emphasized its undoubted relevance. *Bingaman v. State-II,* 76 P.3d 398, 408–9 (Alaska App. 2003). Moreover, Alaska courts have made clear that the risk of countervailing unfair prejudice is categorically *less* where, as here, the accused is the proponent, instead of the subject, of the other-crimes evidence. *See Jordan v. State,* 895 P.2d 994, 999 (Alaska App. 1995); *Garner v. State,* 711 P.2d 1191, 1195 n.3 (Alaska App. 1986).

16. In *Smithart II,* the witness's prior consensual sexual conduct with a fifteen-year-old girl was held not probative of whether the witness raped and killed the twelve-year-old victim in the instant case. 988 P.2d, 590 n.35. Because the consensual conduct was fundamentally and qualitatively dissimilar, it was properly excluded.

17. The proffered evidence consisted of the testimony of two witnesses who had observed the neighbor lose control when her child cried, leading to her shaking and/or hitting her child to the point where the witnesses feared for the child's safety. *Garner v. State,* 711 P.2d, 1193. Although there was testimony that police had investigated reports of abuse committed by the neighbor, apparently none resulted in prosecution. *Id.,* 1194.

Garner had no motive theory to explain why the neighbor would have abused his stepson, but he was able to show that his neighbor had access to his stepson, and thus opportunity to commit the crime, on the day that the fatal injury was inflicted. *Id.,* 1192, 1194. The trial judge permitted defense counsel to cross-examine the neighbor about abusing her own child but precluded the defense from calling its eyewitnesses after the neighbor flatly denied committing such abuse. *Id.,* 1193–94. The jury convicted Garner of manslaughter.

Reversing this conviction, the Court of Appeals held that the trial judge abused his discretion by excluding the evidence. *Garner,* 711 P.2d., 1195. In *Smithart-II,* the Supreme Court summarized, and adopted, the legal basis for the *Garner* holding—

> The court of appeals reversed Garner's manslaughter conviction, holding that the trial court should have admitted alternative-perpetrator evidence under *Marrone,* notwithstanding that the evidence against [the neighbor] was quite weak—she had no motive to kill [appellant's stepson] and the evidence against her was prior-bad-acts evidence, which is generally disfavored. Because [the neighbor] had the opportunity to commit the crime and had abused children in the past, the court of appeals reasoned that a jury could reasonably infer that she had abused [appellant's stepson] as well, an inference that could easily lead a jury to conclude that there existed a reasonable doubt about Garner's guilt. And because identity was the central issue in the case, the trial court's refusal to admit the evidence implicated Garner's right to fully present his defense.

Smithart v. State-II, 988 P.2d, 587–88. Here, as in *Garner,* identity is plainly the "central" issue.

Additionally, where the accused offers other-suspect evidence "against witnesses who testify against him at trial," his entitlement is even stronger than in cases where the other-suspect is not a testimonial accuser at trial. *Smithart v. State II,* 988 P.2d, 588.[18]

Finally, the Alaska Supreme Court emphasizes that the evidentiary issue of the admissibility of other-suspect evidence must be decided in the context of, and with considerable deference to, the accused's constitutional right to present his defense. *Smithart II,* 988 P.2d, 585–86, 588 & 591. See Sec. I.G., *infra.*[19]

Here, the following facts more than satisfy the legal standard for admission of other-suspect evidence:

- Sucha Snitch spontaneously confessed to Officer Krupke that he stabbed Quarrel Kwiktrigger four times.
- Sucha Snitch still admits his presence and participation in the store.

18. *Accord State v. Hawkins,* 260 N.W.2d, 158 (Minn. 1977), *quoted* in *Smithart v. State-II,* 988 P.2d, 588–89. The Confrontation Clause ramifications of such a situation are apparent. *See generally Olden v. Kentucky,* 488 U.S. 227 (1988); *Davis v. Alaska,* 415 U.S. 308 (1974); *Chambers v. Mississippi,* 410 U.S. 284, 295 (1973).
19. *Accord Keith v. State,* 612 P.2d 977, 982–83 (Alaska 1980) (murder reversed); *Shepard v. State,* 847 P.2d 75, 83 (Alaska App. 1993) (manslaughter reversed); *Beagel v. State,* 813 P.2d 699, 708 (Alaska App. 1991) (manslaughter reversed); *Garner v. State,* 711 P.2d 1191, 1195 n.3 (Alaska App. 1986) (manslaughter reversed).

- Sucha Snitch swears only two people were involved in the stabbing/robbery.
- Sucha Snitch fits the description Kwiktrigger gave of the robber who first entered the store with another, scar-faced person.
- Quarrel Kwiktrigger described the person with Sucha Snitch as older, tall, light-skinned, and with a scar running down the right side of his face.
- Quarrel Kwiktrigger insists Scarface was present as a lookout.
- Sucha Snitch and Scarface robbed Sucha Snitch's teacher two years earlier.
- Sucha Snitch had and used a knife to rob his teacher.
- Another teen stood lookout.
- This lookout was an older, tall, light-skinned teen with a scar running down the right side of his face.
- Although Sucha Snitch was arrested, questioned about, and admitted being involved in both robberies, he refuses to admit the existence or identity of his lookout.

This evidence, taken together, at least tends to raise a reasonable doubt as to Mr. Piper's guilt. Accordingly, evidence of Sucha and Scarface's knifepoint robbery of the teacher two years ago is admissible. *Smithart v. State-II,* 988 P.2d, 587.

E. Even When the **Smithart-II** *Standard Is Not Met, the Defense Is Entitled to Argue Reasonable Inferences, from Otherwise Admissible Evidence, That Particular Persons May Have Committed the Crimes Charged*

The *Smithart-II* standard, discussed in Sec. I.D., *supra,* addresses the admissibility of extrinsic evidence tending to show that some other-suspect may have committed the charged offense. If the defense does not satisfy that standard, then extrinsic evidence tending to implicate the other-suspect is not admissible on that ground alone. However, nothing in law prevents the defense from identifying and arguing the culpability of specific other-suspects, in opening statement and/or closing argument, based on evidence that will be, or has been, admitted at trial for other purposes. The *Smithart-I* court made this very point in a two-step analysis, with which the Supreme Court agreed in *Smithart-II.*

First, the Court of Appeals held that an accused's failure to satisfy the other-suspect evidence admissibility standard does not preclude admission of the evidence for other purposes, such as to show the occurrence of relevant conduct, witness bias, or other impeachment.

> [W]hen evidence is primarily relevant for a different purpose, [the other-suspect standard] does not require exclusion of the evidence simply because it might also have the subsidiary effect of suggesting that someone else committed the crime.

Smithart I, 946 P.2d, 1278.

Second, the Court held that the defense is entitled to argue any and all rational inferences from the evidence—including other-suspect inferences. *Smithart-I,* 946 P.2d, 1279, 1281.

The Alaska Supreme Court subsequently approved this analysis regarding the right to argue other-suspect inferences from evidence admitted for other purposes, both in opening statement and in closing argument.

Nothing in *Marrone* limits an attorney from using an opening statement or closing summation to draw reasonable inferences about a third party's involvement from trial evidence. The Court of Appeals correctly explained that, under *Marrone, Smithart* should have been able to argue to the jury that [state witness DeForest] was guilty of the charged crimes:

> [T]he *Marrone* rule limits the introduction of evidence, but it does not limit a party's ability to argue all reasonable inferences from the evidence that is admitted. If, despite *Marrone*'s restriction on the introduction of independent evidence that DeForest committed the crime, it was clear that sufficient evidence would be introduced at Smithart's trial to warrant a reasonable inference that DeForest might be the perpetrator, then Smithart would be entitled to announce this inference in his opening statement.

Smithart-II, 988 P.2d, 589 & *Smithart-I,* 946 P.2d, 1281.

Thus, "[a] party is allowed to argue any inference that can be fairly drawn from the evidence." *Smithart-I,* 946 P.2d, 1279, 1281.[20]

Certainly, counsel for the accused must be permitted at least as much leeway in arguing evidence and inferences as that accorded to the prosecutor. If anything, the accused's right to present evidence and to argue it to the jury is broader than the prosecutor's range of advocacy, because the accused holds specific constitutional guarantees—confrontation, due process, compulsory process, and the effective assistance of counsel. As the Alaska Supreme Court recently held, "the right to argue in one's own defense is a fundamental component of the right to a fair criminal trial." *Smithart-II,* 988 P.2d, 591.

Thus, admission of the proffered evidence for any of the reasons discussed in Secs. I.A.–C. permits the defense to argue the other-suspect inferences regarding Sucha Snitch and Scarface.

20. Prior to *Smithart-I & II,* the case law on the argue-any-rational-inference principle largely addressed the propriety of prosecutors' jury arguments. *See, e.g., Dorman v. Alaska,* 622 P.2d 448, 461 (Alaska 1981); *Gafford v. State,* 440 P.2d 405, 414 (Alaska 1968), *overruled in part on other grounds; Fields v. State,* 487 P.2d 831 (Alaska 1971); *Bentley v. State,* 393 P.2d 225, 230 (Alaska 1964); *Anderson v. State,* 384 P.2d 669, 674 (1963). In this context, prosecutor arguments "need only be within the range of reasonable inference which could be drawn from the evidence." *Dorman v. Alaska,* 622 P.2d, 641. Inferences may be argued when they are "within the record or fairly deducible therefrom." *Gafford v. State,* 440 P.2d, 414; *Anderson v. State,* 384 P.2d, 674. Argument is permitted so long as it has "a basis in the evidence." *Bentley v. State,* 393 P.2d, 230. The only pre-*Smithart I* case addressing the issue in the context of a defense argument is *Sam v. State,* 842 P.2d 596, 601–2 (Alaska App. 1992). *Sam* simply held that defense counsel could not intentionally argue to the jury evidence that had not been admitted for any purpose.

F. ARE 403 Favors Admission of Defense 404(b)(1) Evidence

Properly applied, ARE 403 authorizes easier admission of prior misconduct evidence when the accused is the proponent and a state witness is the subject of the evidence. *Jordan v. State,* 895 P.2d 994, 999 (Alaska App. 1995).

Indeed, in *Garner v. State,* 711 P.2d 1191, 1195 n.3 (Alaska App. 1986), the court used this rationale to help support its reversal of a child-homicide conviction, because of the trial court's erroneous exclusion of evidence that the defendant's neighbor had previously beaten a different child.[21]

Accordingly, the reduced risk of unfair prejudice inherent in prior misconduct evidence offered regarding a witness lightens that side of the Rule 403 balance and further supports admission of the proffered evidence.

G. The Constitutional Entitlement to Prove Innocence

Both the state and federal Constitutions entitle the accused to confront the witnesses against him, to compel the presence of witnesses on his behalf, and to a process that is fundamentally fair. Art. I, §§ 7 & 11, Alaska Constitution; Amendments VI & XIV, U.S. Constitution; *Chambers v. Mississippi,* 410 U.S. 284, 295 (1973). Compulsory process means more than procuring a witness's presence at trial. To "protect the integrity of the adversary

21. *Accord Keith v. State,* 612 P.2d 977 (Alaska 1980) (decedent's journal admissible to show volatile state of mind).

process," that provision includes "the right to have the witness' testimony heard by the trier of fact." *Taylor v. Illinois,* 484 U.S. 400 (1988); *Rock v. Arkansas,* 483 U.S. 44, 51–53 (1987).

Taken together, the rights to compulsory process, confrontation, and due process guarantee the accused his right to present "a defense as we know it." *California v. Green,* 399 U.S. 149, 176 (1970) (Harlan J., concurring). See also *Westen, Confrontation and Compulsory Process: A Unified Theory of Evidence in Criminal Cases,* 91 Harv. L. Rev. 567 (1978).

In reversing a murder conviction, the Alaska Supreme Court expounded on the accused's right to defend—

> Although not absolute, a defendant's right to present a defense is a fundamental element of due process. When a trial court's evidentiary rulings substantially infringe upon the right to present a defense, the court necessarily violates the defendant's due process rights. . . .
>
> [The trial court's rulings] robbed Smithart's case of its cohesion and narrative force and impaired his right to present his own defense. Defendants are "entitled to present [their] version of the events and the evidence supporting it in as full a manner as possible."

Smithart v. State, 988 P.2d 583, 586, 591 (Alaska 1999).[22] *Accord Keith v. State,* 612 P.2d 977, 982–83 (Alaska 1980). Therefore,

22. The Court of Appeals also enforces the accused's right to defend. Reversing a manslaughter conviction in *Shepard v. State,* 847 P.2d 75, 83 (Alaska App. 1993), the Court said, "[W]e consider it significant that the accused's right to present evidence at trial finds expression in the due process and compulsory process clauses of the United States Constitution. . . . The fundamental

where an accused's constitutional entitlement to present his defense conflicts with evidentiary rules, the constitutional mandate requires the court to permit the introduction of evidence that, if offered by the state, would properly be excluded.[23]

Conclusion

For the reasons presented above, Mr. Piper is entitled, as a matter of evidentiary and constitutional law, to present evidence of Sucha and Scarface's knifepoint robbery of the teacher two years ago.

Dated at Anytown, Alaska, this ___ day of ___, 0000.

Respectfully submitted,

Etc.

---

nature of the right counsels strongly against its grudging and parsimonious application." *Accord Beagel v. State,* 813 P.2d 699, 708 (Alaska App. 1991) (manslaughter reversed; precluded "expert testimony critical to [] defense.").

23. *Rock v. Arkansas,* 483 U.S. 44 (1987) (accused's posthypnotic testimony); *Chambers v. Mississippi,* 410 U.S. 284 (1973) (witness voucher rule); *Smithart v. State-II,* 988 P.2d 583, 586, 591 (Alaska 1999) (other-suspect evidence); *Garner v. State,* 711 P.2d 1191, 1194 (Alaska App. 1986) (other-suspect's bad acts). *See* also *U.S. v. Scheffer,* 523 U.S. 303, 318 (Kennedy, O'Connor, Ginsburg & Breyer, J. J., concurring), 331–32 & nn. 18 & 19 (Stevens, J., dissenting) (1998) (doubting/rejecting validity of per se exclusion of polygraph evidence to show accused's consciousness of innocence).

Appendix G

Trapdoor-Closing Elements Jury Instruction

Following is an example showing that just a few words in a jury instruction can make the difference between conviction and acquittal in a high-profile murder case. I tried this case with Ms. Strout, and a critical portion of the cross-examination of one of the key state witnesses is contained in appendix B of *Dynamic Cross-Examination.*

Due to Case Analysis prior to trial, we anticipated the existence of a trapdoor, because of the case's ugliness and high community profile. Our client was indicted and tried as the sole principal. We believed that the jury could find the evidence that our client personally killed the decedent to be insufficient. However, we feared that the jury would still speculate that the accused played some other unidentified and unproven role in the murder, resulting in his conviction.

Accordingly, at the end of trial, we requested special language in the causation part of the standard Murder-1 elements instruction, as well as in all of the lesser included offense instructions. The special language we sought and received is in boldface in the following instruction on the elements of Murder-1. Calling it unnecessary, given the addition in the Murder-1 charge, the Court declined to insert the same special "caused the death means . . ." language in the Murder-2, Manslaughter, and Criminally Negligent Homicide elements instructions.

Any special language may seem unnecessary to some. The whole multimonth trial focused on the question: who was the killer? The state claimed our client acted alone. There was no evidence anyone ever aided and abetted anyone else. For our part, we had four specific and unrelated other-suspects who could have done the murder.

But real jury dynamics are different from case summaries. The didn't-kill-her-but-somehow-involved trapdoor could come into play as the jurors grappled with the difficulty of returning a public acquittal in such a brutal, high-profile case.

It turns out, our Case Analysis of trapdoors, and resultant modification of the causation portion of the Murder-1 instruction, were right on target. Five days into deliberations, the jury sent a note asking if it had to find that the accused himself personally killed the decedent to be guilty of Murder-2. The judge reread the relevant special language from the Murder-1 instruction to them and explained that it applied to every homicide charge before them.

Fifteen minutes later, the jury's note asked, "Do you mean that to convict him of any level of homicide, we must find he is the one who hit her in the head with the rock?" Consistent with the instructions, the judge responded, "If you find that the decedent was killed by being hit in the head with a rock, you may not convict the defendant of any level of homicide, unless you also find, beyond a reasonable doubt, that he is the one who hit her in the head with the rock."

Half an hour later, the jury acquitted our client of Murder-1 and of all its lesser included homicide offenses.

Copy with Supporting Authority for the Judge

JURY INSTRUCTION NO. __

[ELEMENTS OF MURDER-1]

First degree murder is committed when a person causes the death of another person, without legal justification or excuse, and with the intent to cause that death.

In order to find the defendant guilty of first degree murder, the state must prove to you each and every one of the following propositions, beyond a reasonable doubt:

First, that the events leading to the death of Darla Decedent occurred on or about ______,_____ in or about Anytown, America;

Second, that the defendant caused the death of Ms. Decedent. **In this case, "caused the death" means that the defendant personally killed Ms. Decedent;**

[This is the critical trapdoor closing sentence, which was added to the pattern instruction.]

Third, that the defendant intended to kill Ms. Decedent.

[This language was used instead of the standard "another human being," because there was no conceivable issue of transferred intent.]

If you find that each and every one of these propositions is proven beyond a reasonable doubt, then you shall find the defendant guilty of Murder in the First Degree.

However, if you find that any of these propositions is not proven beyond a reasonable doubt, then you must find the defendant not guilty of Murder in the First Degree.

Clean Copy for the Jury

INSTRUCTION NO. ___

First degree murder is committed when a person causes the death of another person, without legal justification or excuse, and with the intent to cause that death.

In order to find the defendant guilty of first degree murder, the state must prove to you each and every one of the following propositions, beyond a reasonable doubt:

First, that the events leading to the death of Darla Decedent occurred on or about ______,_____ in or about Anytown, America;

Second, that the defendant caused the death of Ms. Decedent. In this case, "caused the death" means that the defendant personally killed Ms. Decedent;

Third, that the defendant intended to kill Ms. Decedent.

If you find that each and every one of these propositions is proven beyond a reasonable doubt, then you shall find the defendant guilty of Murder in the First Degree.

However, if you find that any of these propositions is not proven beyond a reasonable doubt, then you must find the defendant not guilty of Murder in the First Degree.

Index

G

H

I

J

K

About the Author

Jim McComas defended people accused of the most serious crimes for thirty years, in both state and federal courts.

After graduating from Harvard Law School in 1978, Jim worked as a trial and appellate attorney at The Public Defender Service, Washington, DC. In 1983, he was appointed training director, and from 1984 to 1986, Jim was Chief of the Trial Division.

In 1986, Jim went into private practice. He ended up trying and, after a mistrial, retrying a notorious contract murder case two winters in a row in Fairbanks, Alaska. Following his client's acquittal in 1988, Jim and his family moved to Anchorage.

Jim's practice focused on homicide cases. He defended Alaskans accused of murder in many trials, lasting from three weeks to more than three months, and usually ending in acquittals.

Jim helped create, and for four years was president of, Alaskans against the Death Penalty, devoting about a quarter of his time to that cause. In 1995, the Alaska Civil Liberties Union named him Civil Libertarian of the Year.

In 2001, Jim represented a public defender targeted by a bad-faith prosecution. The fee was $10, but the work was full-time for nine months. Judge Link's fifty-page order remains one of the few written decisions finding that prosecutors acted in actual, institutional bad faith. In May 2002, Jim became the first recipient of the annual Jim McComas Alaskan Champion of Liberty Award, created by the Alaska Academy of Trial Lawyers and the Alaska Criminal Defense Bar.

Throughout his career, Jim also wrote, prepared, and presented CLEs, intensive training programs, and initial public defender training programs, lasting from one day to six weeks.

In 2008, Jim and his wife, Anne, a public school speech-language pathologist, retired. They live on the banks of the Turtle-Flambeau Flowage in far northern Wisconsin. Jim is also the author of *Dynamic Cross-Examination: A Whole New Way to Create Opportunities to Win.*